RELOCATION 101:

FOCUS ON THE GREATER VANCOUVER AREA

BY

Janet Auty-Carlisle & Kai Hansen

The book for people Relocating to Vancouver B.C., Canada

D1392321

Printed simulatanously around the world by BOOKSURGE (Canada, US, UK, NL, AU, ES, EU) http://www.booksurge.com

National Library of Canada Cataloguing in Publication Data

Auty-Carlisle, Janet 1956 -

Relocation 101: focus on the Greater Vancouver area

Includes index.

ISBN:

1. Moving, Household -- British Columbia -- Vancouver Metropolitan Area -- Handbooks, manuals, etc 2. Vancouver Metropolitan Area (B.C.) -- Guide-books

I. Hansen, Kai, 1943 -

II. Title

FC3846.18.A98 2001   971.1'2804   C2001-903957-3

F1089.5.V6A98 2001

CONTENTS

All our contact listings are partial lists only. For a complete
listing consult a yellow pages guide.

All our contact listings are partial lists only. For a complete listing consult a yellow pages guide.

Relocation 101:Focus on the Greater Vancouver Area

would not have been possible without the co-operation between the following two authors.

Janet Auty-Carlisle

To my husband Jim and my children Tara and Liam...We are all presented with different paths and destinations in our lives. Know in your hearts, that no matter the road you choose, all paths lead you home.

And Kai Hansen

Thank you to some very special people: Mary Lovett, Murray and Pearl Fallen and Tom Marcinkiewicz.

Picture Credit:
Grant Fuller Artist, http://www.grantfuller.ca

CHAPTER 1:

Relocation 101:Focus on the Greater Vancouver Area

INTRODUCTION

People move for many reasons, for a new job, a climate change or maybe the family has moved. Perhaps it is the opportunity to start fresh in a new province or country. Whatever the reason, relocating is difficult; change is frightening and stressful.

There is the uncertainty of the unknown...will you fit in, how different is the culture, what are the work habits of your new co-workers like? What do people do for entertainment, where will you live, will your lifestyle and quality of life remain the same or become better or worse than it currently is?

If you are living with a partner you must consider his/her career options. Is he/she willing to give up his/her job in order to support this relocation? Is there a possibility of a position for him/her at your new place of employment, does your company offer career counselling as part of the relocation package?

Relocating to a new destination is very difficult for adults, single or married. The issue becomes much more complicated when children are involved. Not only do you have to contend with the practical issues of educational needs, you must also consider community facilities and support programs.

Relocation 101:Focus on the Greater Vancouver Area provides you with all the details of moving to Vancouver and surrounding areas including important phone numbers, area orientation, orientation map, school and community information.

We have an excellent website for you to visit for updates.

http://relocation101.ca

Enjoy your new city and much success with your new move.

Janet Auty-Carlisle and Kai Hansen

RELOCATION 101

Basically, a relocation works this way. You have been working with your company for some time now, or you are a newly hired employee.

An offer to relocate is presented to you, outlining the proposed job position, initial incentives and basic information. This is the time for deliberation and discussion with family, friends or perhaps co-workers who have had relocation experience in the past.

If you feel this opportunity to relocate is something you should investigate further, make arrangements with your superiors to discuss this in detail. Your human resources department will probably be able to provide you with information relating to the relocation process. You should discuss the benefits and features of the relocation policy being offered to you including such things as housing, allowance, mortgage or rental differentials (if applicable), salary, anticipated duration of the transfer and moving expense coverage.

It is also necessary to discuss, with a specialized human resource person, issues regarding government documents, visas, taxation issues, medical issues and vehicle registrations. The taxation issue can become quite complicated and some corporations out-source this to accredited taxation lawyers. They will assist you in making the best decision financially regarding allowable deductions related to personal income taxation etc.

You should visit the designated city at least once for an orientation or fact-finding trip.

Some details must be taken care of prior to your moving in to your new property. These include contacting the telephone company to have service installed, as well as the cable company for television, hydro (known as electrical power in the United States) water and gas. You will also need to establish a bank account. This can generally be handled through your new corporate destination. Quite often they will have a reciprocal agreement with a specific bank branch for transferees to ensure that you can open an account with ease and avoid the issue of not having an established credit rating in this new city.

If you have arranged to have painting or cleaning done in your new residence, be sure it is done prior to moving in your furniture. It is much easier, less mess and a better job can be done.

The new position will offer you an opportunity to meet new people and gain new work experience. This is also a great networking opportunity to find out where the best entertainment areas are, restaurants, bars, sport clubs etc.

Keep in mind that if you are moving with a partner or family, they may feel quite isolated at this time. It is important that they be introduced to the newcomers club or similar club in your area. Perhaps volunteer work is the answer to the inevitable loneliness or an opportunity to return to academic upgrading. You may not have the same feeling of alienation because you will have your work to keep you occupied but be prepared for some negative feedback from your partner/spouse.

We have discussed the issue of relocating from your current location to a new location. There is also the need to take into consideration your reintegration or repatriation into your
current location when you return.

There are several stages that people tend to go through when they find out they are returning "home." Initially, there is a sense of euphoria, happiness to be going back to someplace familiar. Sadness at leaving all the new people and places that you have become accustomed to at your new place. Feeling isolated upon the return to the original location because people have changed and life has managed to go on without you. Things are not as they were when you left and you can't return and simply pick up the pieces where you left off. This is a very disconcerting feeling for many people and can be quite a shock.

Quite often home doesn't feel like home anymore. The home you knew is more of an emotional attachment to happy memories and events that took place there. You may feel like a foreigner in your own place upon your return. Remember, you've been away for a long time and much has changed.

Besides the emotional issues, there are some practical issues that will have to be handled. You will have to arrange for movers again, forwarding mail, closing bank accounts, disconnecting cable, gas, water, telephone and hydro.

If there are children involved they will have to readjust to a school system that they left many years ago. Some children find this very traumatic, depending on the age group and life situation.

A Relocation "Survivor" Story featuring the Taylor Family

Meet the Taylor family. They are a family of 5, father, mother and three children. The father is an executive with a global firm and the family has relocated many times. His wife is not eligible to work in Canada but she can volunteer. Their three children are accustomed to attending private, international schools.
This is their story.

ON SETTLING IN

"Having been an expat for 5 years prior to moving to Canada, I guess one has certain expectations of how easy it will be or indeed difficult.You expect to take three months to settle in, meet new friends, sort out your unpacking and get on with life."

"Canada is a beautiful country and we loved our time here. Knowing what to expect ahead of time would have been very beneficial. An example of this was the newcomers clubs. It took us almost a year to discover this organization and get involved in the community. Other issues were tackled in an ad hoc fashion, which could have been avoided with information about our new area prior to the move."

ON HOUSING

"With a low vacancy rate in some urban areas, it can be stressful finding suitable accommodation. The rental market inventory is so small, the race to secure a property is won by the fast and those whose company lawyers are poised, literally hour by hour, to approve lease contracts."

ON DRIVING

"In the province we moved to we were surprised to find out that only U.S. and Japanese transferees could exchange a drivers license without having to take their G2 test. For any other drivers, even with many years of driving experience, the G2 test was mandatory. Technically this means one cannot drive at night or on the expressways until passing the G2 test. This can take some time to arrange."

The ministries of transportation governing such rules are provincially established governments and so, rules of the road vary from province to province.

SUMMARY

"It's a very strange paradox that, given the historical connections with Europe, moving to Canada is such a challenge to expats."

"The travel and holidays, drives to Nova Scotia, brilliant skiing in Alberta and British Columbia and camping in the national parks have made this relocation worthwhile."

"Having a guide such as Relocation 101 would have been very useful."

I. Taylor and family, March 2002

ORIENTATION MAP OF GREATER VANCOUVER

More Vancouver Mapping on the Internet:

WEB: http://relocatecanada.com/mapping.html

http://www.tourism-vancouver.org/docs/maps/

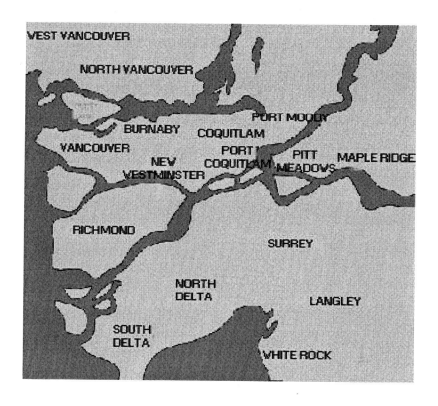

CHAPTER 2:

FACTS AT A GLANCE

CANADA	BRITISH COLUMBIA	VANCOUVER
• history	• history	• history
• population	• population	• population
• government	• government	• government
• geography	• geography	• geography
• health care	• health care	• weather
• national symbols	• weather	• ethnic diversity

CANADA

HISTORY

The name Canada is derived from an Iroquois name. Jacques Cartier, an early French explorer, made note that Iroquois Indians referred to an area near the city of Quebec as "kanata." The English translation of "kanata"is a cluster of buildings. The navigation maps and charts Cartier prepared designated the area to be called Kanata, which later became Canada.

Canada was first discovered by Norse explorers in the tenth century. A small settlement was established on the northern tip of Newfoundland which is known today as L'Anse aux Meadows. Venetian explorers, under the leadership of King Henry VII landed in Newfoundland in the year 1497. John Cabot was the captain of this exploration team.

By the late 1500's the area was pronounced to be an English colony. Jacques Cartier founded the city of Quebec in the early 1500's and pronounced it to be a French colony. Many centuries of unrest would follow between the French and British governments in an effort to establish ownership of various territories.

In the year 1759 the dominance of one country over another was established by the infamous Plains of Abraham battle which took place in the city of Quebec. General James Wolfe of the British army attacked the fortresses of the French army. Louis Montcalm who was a general for the French army had managed to defend the fortress for most of the summer but Wolfe planned a surprise evening attack on the French troops. In the ensuing battle both Montcalm and Wolfe were mortally wounded. The French troops could not bring reinforcements in with this fortress now out of their posession. This ultimately led to their surrender to the British troops. The British flag would fly over the fortress by the end of 1763.

POPULATION

The population of Canada is aproximately 30 million people. The majority of the population is centred around the regions of Southern Ontario, Vancouver and Montreal.

Canada is a multi-cultural country as is reflected in the population of visible minorities. Aproximately three million people, or 10% of the total population are considered visible minorities. British Columbia has the largest population of visible minorities (18%) with Ontario as a close second (16%.) The largest group of visible minorities consist of Chinese people in both cities.

GOVERNMENT

The British North-America Act, established on July 1, 1867 embodied the written constitutional act of Canada for well over a century. The original members of this group included the provinces of Ontario, Quebec, New Brunswick and Nova Scotia. Other provinces could join later if they wished.

Each province would have its own seat of government, its own policymaking delegates and its own lieutenant governor. The lieutenant governor is the provincial Canadian representative to the British Crown. The British North-America act also established a federal government which would include elected House of Commons officials, a Senate (appointed for life) and a governor-general.

The governor-general is the federal Canadian representative to the British Crown. The federal government established the matters on which the provinces could make laws and those which would be of special concern and remain under the federal government parties to this day. The government of Canada was officially recognized on November 6, 1867. Sir. John A. Macdonald was the first prime minister and led the country under a conservative banner.

The two official governments were the Liberal party and the Conservative party. Macdonald led the parliament until his defeat in 1873 by Alexander Mackenzie, head of the Liberal party. The official, elected head of the country is known as the Prime Minister.

The Liberals and Conservatives continue to be the dominant parties to this day. Altenative parties such as the New Democratic Party, the Parti Quebecois and the Alliance Party continue to make inroads with the Canadian public and gain more seats in the federal house of Parliament.

GEOGRAPHY

• The capital of Canada is Ottawa, in Ontario.
• Canada is made up of ten provinces and three territories.
• Canada covers 9,978,653 square kilometers (3,851,790 square miles). This makes it the second largest country in the world behind Russia.
• The world's largest lake, Lake Superior, is bordered by both Canada and the United States

HEALTH CARE

Health care is availabe to all Canadians as established by the federal government's Canada Health Act. Health care insurance plans have basic similarities across the country including coverage of "medically necessary" hospital services and the services of a physician, however, any further coverage varies from province to province based on additional provincial funding.

NATIONAL SYMBOLS

The Canadian flag is a red maple leaf on a white background with a red band on each end. White represents the snowy north of Canada, red symbolizes the Canadian blood shed during World War 1 and the stylized maple leaf has been Canada's national symbol for over 150 years. This became the official flag of Canada on February 15, 1965.

• The national plant is the Maple Leaf.
• The national animal is the Candian Beaver.
• The national sport officially is Lacrosse.
• The national sport unofficially is Hockey.
• The national anthem is O'Canada.

BRITISH COLUMBIA

HISTORY

British Columbia entered the Dominion of Canada on July 20, 1871. In 1774, Spanish explorers visited the area now known as British Columbia.

While the English and French were fighting over territory in eastern Canada Spain and Russia were the first countries to claim ownership of certain parts of British Columbia. The Spanish claimed the west coast of North America from Mexico to Vancouver Island in the 18th century. During this same time period the Russians were also making an effort to claim control of the Pacific coast from Alaska to San Francisco. Captain James Cook, a British explorer, became the first person to map out the region of British Columbia. Victoria would become the first permanent colony, established by the British in 1843. The gold rush of 1857 caused the population of Victoria and other regions of British Columbia to soar. The British government established the colony of British Columbia in 1858 and by 1871 they had joined forces with the Dominion of Canada.

POPULATION

The population of British Columbia is aproximately 3,029,000. 79% of the people reside in urban areas and 21% reside in rural areas. English is the main language used in British Columbia with an average of 81% of the population having English as a first language. Chinese and Southeast Asian languages are the first languages used by 15% of the population. The majority of B.C.'s inhabitants are of British origin.More than 100,000 British Columbians are descendants of the Chinese immigrant workers who took part in the construction of the Canadian Pacific Railway in the late 19th century.

GOVERNMENT

The province of British Columbia is led by the premier. The premier is an elected official. He/she is voted into office through general elections held every four years (or less.) His/her mandate includes such issues as provincial health, education, transportation, child and family development, forestry, provincial development and provincial revenues. The premier's party caucus sit in the House of Commons which in located in Victoria, the capital of British Columbia.

There are two official parties in the provincial legislature, the Liberal party and the NDP party. The 301-seat House of Commons and 104-seat Senate in Ottawa include 34 elected Members of Parliament from B.C. and 6 B.C. senators appointed by the federal government.

GEOGRAPHY

- British Columbia is 946,011 square kilometres.
  (365,255 square miles.) in area.
- The capital city is Victoria.
- The provincial motto is Splendor without diminishment.
- The provincial flower is the Pacific dogwood.
- The provincial bird is the Steller's jay.
- The principal products are pulp-and-paper products and lumber. primary minerals processed foods and livestock.
- Canada's highest waterfall, Della Falls is located in Strathcona Park. At 440 metres Della Falls is one of the ten highest falls in the world.

HEALTH CARE

Every resident of British Columbia is entitled to provincial health care, also known as the Medical Services Plan of BC. (MSP) Enrollment with MSP is voluntary. Residents who want coverage for themselves and their dependents must register with MSP. Hospital insurance is provided to all eligible residents of British Columbia.

Pharmacare is the provincial pharmaceutial assistance program. Many prescription drugs are paid for a patient by the pharmacare program.

If you are eligible for benefits during an absence from B.C., MSP will help pay for unexpected medical services you receive anywhere in the world,provided the services are medically required, rendered by a licensed medical practitioner and normally insured by MSP. Reimbursement is made in Canadian funds and does not exceed the amount payable had the same services been performed in B.C.. Any excess cost is the responsibility of the beneficiary.

WEATHER

The climate of British Columbia is influenced by its location immediately east of the Pacific Ocean and the north-south orientation of its towering mountain chains. In winter, the province is affected occasionally by much colder, drier air from the Arctic. During the summer, a weakening in the west to east upper air flow in combination with the development of a persistent high pressure area off the coast results in fewer frontal systems moving through BC. As a result, summers tend to be dry throughout most of BC. The beautiful coast of British Columbia is well known for its temperate climate - the finest in Canada! For weather updates and information, Vancouver has a pay per use telephone number. The Weather-One-on-One service is $2.99 per minute.

Telephone: 1-900-565-5555
WEB: http://weatheroffice.ec.gc.ca/

VANCOUVER

HISTORY

Long before Europeans visited the west coast, diverse Coast Salish groups such as the Tsawwassen, Coquitlam, Katzie, and Stó:lo lived, and still live, in the Greater Vancouver region. The three main nations who lived where Vancouver now sits are the Squamish, an amalgamation of 16 Squamish-speaking tribes; the Musqueam, whose language is Hun'q'umin'um' (the down river Halkomelem dialect); and the Tsleil-Waututh, who also speak Hun'q'umin'um'. Not long ago, it was common for people to speak five or six languages because of the trading, intermarriage and other interactions that occurred between groups in the region.

In 1778 James Cook, the famous British captain, first landed at Friendly Cove in Nootka Sound on the western side of Vancouver Island. In 1790 the Spaniard Manuel Quimper, sailing on the sloop Princesa Real, sailed into the Strait of Juan de Fuca off the southern end of Vancouver Island, landing just west of Victoria.

Fourteen years after sailing here under the leadership of the infamous Captain Cook, Captain George Vancouver, (for whom the city is now named) returned to the Strait of Juan de Fuca.

Captain Vancouver spent the next two years exploring the area with the aim of finding the western end of the elusive "Northwest Passage." The explorers hoped this would help British traders to travel more quickly from England to the Pacific Ocean.

In 1808, Simon Fraser, as part of the the North West Company, navigated 35 days to the Pacific all the way down the river since named after him, passing through many uncharted rapids. David Thompson, again with the North West Company, managed to navigate the entire length of the Columbia River. Fur trading posts were established along the Fraser and the Columbia river which began a period of white settlement in the interior of B.C.

When the North West and Hudson's Bay companies merged in 1821, the province already had significant agricultural interests centered around the forts, providing supplies for travelers, traders and the Royal Navy.

By 1866, the colonies of B.C. and Vancouver Island were united, but an economy based on just fur trading and mining was not stable enough to encourage growth. In 1871, four years after Canada was given it's independence by Britain, B.C. joined the Canadian confederation. The B.C. provincial government began encouraging the agricultural and forestry industries, to begin economic diversification.

Vancouver began as a little log cabin city amongst tall trees (when the whole city looked like the forests in Stanley Park.) In 1866 a devastating fire destroyed much of the Vancouver region. This tragic fire razed over 1000 buildings in 20 minutes due to the strong winds and after the damage was assessed more than 3000 people were left homeless. The early settlers of Vancouver were a determined group and were not going to allow this fire to destroy their dreams. They began the daunting task of rebuilding their beautiful town and eventually became a prosperous community.

On November 7, 1885 the Canadian Pacific Railway set the last spike in its construction at Craigellachie, just east of Shushwap Lake. The first trans-continental railway train arrived, to much fanfare, in Port Moody on July 4, 1886. It took another year to extend the railway 20 kilometres more to go directly into Vancouver.

After the railway connected B.C.'s ports to the rest of Canada, it was only natural to connect Canada to the rest of the world. In 1891 the CPR "Empress of India" was the first CPR ocean liner to arrive from the Orient. In 1904, the Great Northern Railway connected the city to Seattle. The 1914 opening of the Panama Canal made Vancouver an important west coast port.

POPULATION

Vancouver is Canada's third largest city, following Toronto and Montreal, with an area population of 2.6 million. Vancouver City has a population of approximately 450,000.

GOVERNMENT

Vancouver is divided into 21 self-governing municipalities and one electoral area, Anmore, Belcarra, Bowen Island, Burnaby, Coquitlam,Delta and North Delta, Langley, Lions Bay , Maple Ridge, New Westminster, the city of North Vancouver, the district of North Vancouver, Pitt Meadows, Port Coquitlam, Port Moody, Richmond, Surrey, city of Vancouver, district of West Vancouver and Whiterock. These communities combine to form what is known as the Greater Vancouver Regional District.

GEOGRAPHY

The topography in the City of Vancouver ranges from perfectly flat land in the flood plain of the Fraser River to steep-sloped valleys in Pacific Spirit Park and the vertical cliffs at Prospect Point. Rain-fed creeks and small lakes, and the waters of the Pacific Ocean mark Vancouver's blue space.

Vancouver has many popular beaches, the largest being Spanish Banks. Along the southern rim of Vancouver is the Fraser River Estuary, an important stop for migrating birds travelling between Siberia and South America.

WEATHER

Year-round outdoor activities are a part of Vancouver's West Coast Lifestyle. From 24 degrees Celsius (76F) in the summer, to 5 degrees Celsius (41F) in the winter, the climate is always hospitable. Except on the local ski hills, it rarely snows in Vancouver.

ETHNIC DIVERSITY

Chinese immigration to Vancouver began in the late 1800s and continued for many years.

During the 1980s and 1990s the main source of immigration to Vancouver was from the Southeast Asian community, specifically Hong Kong. Many of these immigrants were leaving to escape the economic uncertainty of the hand-over of governments in 1997 from Britain to China.

Vancouver's labour force is the most multilingual in North America. It is not uncommon to hear languages other than English being used as the first language by many immigrant workers.

Over 90 languages are spoken in Greater Vancouver. More than 36% of the population speak languages other than English. Other languages commonly spoken include Chinese, French, Japanese and Punjabi.

26 languages, apart from English, are taught in various universities, colleges, private schools and language centres. Vancouver newspapers are printed in 20 different languages and there are 17 different language stations on Vancouver television.

CHAPTER 3: AREAS

CITY OF VANCOUVER

Vancouver City has a population of aproximately 450,000.

The generic term for Vancouver and its surroundings is the "Lower Mainland" or "Greater Vancouver".

Vancouver is a beautiful city for work, for play and for life; its strikingly beautiful and diverse natural environment provides an excellent setting for all kinds of recreation. Golf, sailing, skiing, year-round jogging, and many other sports provide opportunities for everyone to get out and enjoy the city.

Its climate is one of the mildest in Canada. Temperatures average 3°C in January and 18°C in July. Vancouver's average annual precipitation is 1,219 mm. Most rainfall occurs in winter.

Vancouver is a major port and it is believed to be a world export leader. As the western terminus of Canada's transcontinental highway and rail routes, it is the primary city of western Canada. Vancouver is also the national industrial centre. Major industries include lumber and paper products, shipbuilding, food processing, petroleum refining, hi-tech industries and metal product manufacturing. A superport at Roberts Bank, 40Km to the south is used for exporting coal and ore to Japan.

Vancouver is a major tourist destination. In addition to the city's scenic location, visitors enjoy beautiful gardens and the world - famous Stanley Park. One of the more than 180 city parks, Stanley Park encompasses an area of 1000 acres. Visitors and residents alike enjoy a combination of natural forest and parklands as well as traditional native Totem Poles and a boardwalk around the seawall. Runners, walkers, rollerbladers, cyclists and skateboarders can be seen on the boardwalk at virtually any time of the day or night.

Vancouver residents and visitors also benefit from a wide spectrum of visual and performing artistry. Classical symphonies, opera, theatre, dance companies, and festivals reflect the city's cosmopolitan character and ethnic diversity.

Likewise, Vancouver's social amenities are among the best in North America. Local standards in public education, health, transportation, and personal security are excellent.

There is an extensive bus system and a rapid transit system and also a commuter train service up the Fraser Valley.

The city of Vancouver consists of 23 communities which are described on the following pages.

CONTACT INFORMATION

• City of Vancouver
453 West 12th Ave.
Vancouver, B.C., V5Y 1V4
Telephone: 604-873-7011

The City of Vancouver website will provide you with further information about the city.

WEB: http://www.city.vancouver.bc.ca/

For more information about Vancouver Communities.

WEB: http://www.city.vancouver.bc.ca/community_profiles/

ARBUTUS RIDGE

Arbutus Ridge is a quiet mature area that boasts spectacular views of English Bay and the North Shore mountains. Housing includes up-scale older homes, condominiums and apartments.

• 2001 Population: 14,515

DOWNTOWN

Vancouver is a thriving and growing city. As Canada's third largest city it continues to be the busiest port, a gateway to the Pacific Rim, a transportation terminus, popular tourist destination and centre for business.

Several distinct and unique communties can be found in the city including the infamous Gastown. Gastown is famous for it's night clubs, restaurants and specialty shops. It is an eclectic area that is fre- quented by many local residents.

Chinatown, also centred in downtown Vancouver, provides ethnic character and charm to the community.

• 2001 Population: 27,937

DOWNTOWN EASTSIDE

The downtown Eastside is also a community rich in history, architecture and diversity. This community is one of the oldest in the GVRD.

This area has achieved a certain renown across the country. It has been described as the poorest postal code in Canada. Problems with crime, the homeless and substance abuse have been topics of national discussion.

Despite these issues, many residents take pride in this area and are making a strong effort to maintain the integrity and identity of the Eastside community.

· 2001 Population: 8,880

DUNBAR - SOUTHLANDS

This area is two distinct communities, Dunbar and Southlands. Dunbar is an attractive community of quiet, tree-lined streets, single family homes and beautiful parks.

Southlands is a serene rural community. There seem to be more horses living in Southlands than people.

· 2001 Population: 21,308

FAIRVIEW

Fairview is a family-oriented, inner-city neighbourhood, located near the waterfront. South Granville and Granville Island, two of Vancouver's best shopping districts are in the Fairview area. Granville is home to a large public market with delicious offerings like organic foods, fresh breads, fresh and smoked salmon and eggs.

• 2001 Population: 28,403

GRANDVIEW-WOODLAND

This charismatic area features a diversity of people, housing and land use. The heart of the region is Commercial Drive, a fascinating collection of ethnic restaurants, food stores, funky coffee bars, vintage clothing shops and street buskers. "The Drive" is known throughout the city for its cosmopolitan appeal.

• 2001 Population: 29,085

HASTINGS-SUNRISE

Hastings-Sunrise is a strong family-oriented community. The Pacific National Exhibition first opened it's doors here in 1910.

• 2001 Population: 33,055

KENSINGTON-CEDAR COTTAGE

Another community combined of two historic neighbourhoods. Cedar Cottage was established in 1888 with the purchase of 43 acres of land. Mr. Arthur Wilson purchased this land and started up a nursery business which he called Cedar Cottage Nursery. Kensington was another small village in the area.

The two villages grew and eventually became the community known as Kensington-Cedar Cottage.

• 2001 Population: 44,556

KERRISDALE

Kerrisdale is a mature, well-established suburban community filled with single-family homes on tree-lined streets, a mix of low and high-rise apartments, and a thriving commercial centre along 41st Avenue.

Kerrisdale was settled in 1867 by the McCleery brothers of Ireland. The area was originally their farmland. The area was named Kerrisdale in 1905 by a longtime resident who chose the name after her hometown Kerrydale in Scotland.

• 2001 Population: 14,033

KILLARNEY

Killarney was settled in 1868 by William Rowling. He was a surveyor in the British military. He was the only person to receive a land military grant in Vancouver for his service to the British Empire. The area remained rural farm land until after WWII.

Located in the extreme southeast corner of Vancouver - from East 41st Avenue to the Fraser River and from Boundary Road and Vivian Street - Killarney was the last neighbourhood in Vancouver to be developed. This once rural area has experienced significant residential growth that began in the 1950s and continues to this day.

• 2001 Population: 25,785

KITSILANO

First used as a canning factory for the salmon fisheries. The area remained a summer vacation resort for many years. It is now a popular area for university students and travellers alike who can find affordable living accommodations in the converted older homes.

• 2001 Population: 39,386

MARPOLE

Settled in 1860, Marpole was originally known as Eburne Station after the town's first postmaster and store keeper. In 1916 the area was renamed for CPR General Superintendent Richard Marpole.

• 2001 Population: 39,386

MARPOLE TIDBIT

It is believed the Marpole area was inhabited as far back as 3500 B.C. Two early village sites were discovered in 1889. Tools, weapons and other artifacts were found in what proved to be one of the largest village sites discovered in North America.

MOUNT PLEASANT

One of the most diverse communities in the city of Vancouver. The town was settled by H.V. Edmonds who owned much of the land. The town was named by his wife after her hometown in Ireland. Olympic sprinter Percy Williams was from Mount Pleasant. During the 1928 Olympic Games, he took home gold medals in the 100-metre and 200-metre dashes.

- 2001 Population: 24,539

OAKRIDGE

The CPR developed its land holdings in this area in the 1950s for residential and commercial use. Until this time the area remained rural. Residential construction continued into the 1960s as Oakridge became a community for young families. Today the area is a popular suburban neighbourhood.

- 2001 Population: 11,793

RENFREW-COLLINGWOOD

In 1878, George Wales, the earliest settler, bought 221 acres of land in this area. The name Collingwood originated with some of the principals from theTramway company who had previously resided in Collingwood, Ontario.The area was frequently coupled with its neighbour to the north, Renfrew, hence the name Renfrew-Collingwood.

- 2001 Population: 44,946

X-FILE
The 1946 2400 Motel on Kingsway near Nanaimo is a popular film location and has been used in an episode of the X-files.

RILEY PARK

Riley Park is the home of Antique Row. This interesting shopping area is filled with antique shops, unique second-hand stores, and curio shops. Who knows what treasures may be found there. Perhaps a future submission to the Antique Road Show.

- 2001 Population: 21,998

SHAUGHNESSY

Developed by the Canadian Pacific Railway in 1909 as an exclusive community, Shaughnessy is still one of the city's most stable and prosperous communities. The area is named after the fiirst CPR president Sir Thomas Shaughnessy and is characterized by large, well-tended homes on winding, tree-lined streets.

• 2001 Population: 9,012

MORTGAGE HEIGHTS

During the depression, when many Shaughnessy residents lost their homes, the area was referred to as Poverty Hill and Mortgage Heights.

SOUTH CAMBIE

Settled in 1874 by William Mackie a local logger and gold miner. The area became a residential community in the early 1900's. The town is named after yet another CPR employee, engineer Henry Cambie.

• 2001 Population: 6,996

LITTLE MOUNTAIN

Little Mountain,the highest point in Vancouver, occupies its geographical centre and commands a 360-degree view of the entire city.

STRATHCONA

A diverse neighbourhood that has housed a succession of immigrants including British, Irish, Russian, Croatian, Scandinavians, Greeks, Japanese and Chinese who lived here before moving on to other parts of the city. Lord Strathcona School, built in 1897, is one of the of the oldest remaining school buildings in Vancouver.

• 2001 Population: 11,573

VICTORIA-FRASERVIEW

Victoria-Fraserview overlooks the Fraser River and has some of Vancouver's best southern views. Settled in the 1860s this area remained undeveloped until the end of WWII. Returning war veterans created a shortage of housing and so many new communities were built. Victoria-Fraserview was one of those.

• 2001 Population: 27,152

DIAPER TOWN
In the early 1950s, Fraserview became known as "diaper town" because there were so many children in the new subdivision.

SUNSET

Sunset was one of the earliest communities to be settled in the Vancouver area. Originally known as South Vancouver and locally as South Hill, the area's current name dates from 1967, following the naming of Sunset Nurseries, Sunset Park, and the Sunset Community Centre.

• 2001 Population: 33,423

CELEBRITY OPENING
Sunset Community Centre was opened by Bing Crosby in the 1950s.

WEST END

The first settler, John Morton, a potter by trade. Originally living in New Westminster, Morton was interested in the local deposits of coal and clay. Although coal was never actively mined in the area, this discovery led Morton and two partners to lay claim to the land with the intention of establishing a brick making operation.

• 2001 Population: 42,154

The popular Robson Street shopping area is known throughout the city as the place to "see and be seen." It is a major tourist destination and is filled with upscale boutiques, trendy clothing stores, restaurants and coffee shops. Denman Street is another popular shopping haunt, lined with funky shops, inexpensive dining, movie theatres, and the local community centre and library.

The downtown business core is just minutes away, making this area an ideal home for office workers and the many Vancouverites who enjoy the luxury of not needing a car to get around.

WEST POINT GREY

Named in 1792 after Captain George Vancouver's friend Captain George Grey.

The area offers beach-front living, a strong sense of community and great views of the city's skyline and the North Shore mountains. The province's largest university, University of British Columbia, is nearby. The Museum of Anthropology and the huge Pacific Spirit Park are popular tourist spots.

• 2001 Population: 12,911

GOLFING

The Vancouver Golf Club, established in 1892 was the first golf course west of Mississippi. The players used tomato cans for holes.

CITY OF VANCOUVER CONTACT INFORMATION

• City of Vancouver
453 West 12th Avenue, Vancouver, BC, V5Y 1V4
Telephone: 604-873-7011
WEB: http://www.city.vancouver.bc.ca/

THE GREATER VANCOUVER REGIONAL DISTRICT (GVRD)

The first meeting of the GVRD's Board of Directors was on July 12, 1967. At that time, there were 950,000 people living in the region, today there are 2.0 million, and that number is increasing every year.

GVRD delivers essential utility services to residents regionally rather than through a local venue. These utilities include drinking water, sewage treatment and garbage disposal. The GVRD was created out of economic necessity,

The GVRD is divided into 11 departments, whose staff serve all the various boards and committees and the member municipalities. These departments, all of which have separate but connected responsibilities, are linked by a shared vision and common goals.

• 2001 Population: 1,986,965

CONTACT INFORMATION

• Greater Vancouver Regional District GVRD
4330 Kingsway, Burnaby, B.C., V5H 4G8
Telephone: 604-432-6200
Fax Line: 604-432-6251
WEB: http://www.gvrd.bc.ca/

VILLAGE OF ANMORE

The village of Anmore is a small, prisitine region snuggled between Eagle Mountain and the east shore of Indian Arm. The Anmore Valley area has managed to retain its rural character, even as nearby Vancouver continues development and urban growth. The residents of Anmore valley enjoy many outdoor features including horseback riding, canoeing, camping, fishing, recreational diving and hiking.

Anmore is the birthplace of the Greenpeace Environmental Group. Founded by two residents of Anmore, Hal Weinberg, who is the current mayor of Anmore and Bob Hunter, a journalist now residing in Toronto.

• 2001 Population: 1,344

CONTACT INFORMATION

2697 Sunnyside Road, Anmore, B.C., V3H 3C8
Telephone: 604-469- 9877
WEB: http://www.anmore.com/

VILLAGE OF BELCARRA

Epitomizing the relaxed West Coast lifestyle, this well wooded residential community overlooks the magnificent North Shore mountains and the picturesque waters of Indian Arm (which includes Bedwell Bay, Belcarra Bay, Cosy Cove, Whiskey Cove, Farrer Cove and Twin Islands). The residents of Belcarra enjoy a superb natural setting in this quaint village.

Household incomes are amongst the highest in the GVRD.

Belcarra is located 28 kilometres (18 miles) from downtown Vancouver.

• Population: 700

CONTACT INFORMATION

• Village Office
4084 Bedwell Bay Road, Belcarra, B.C., V3H 4P8
Telephone: 604-937-4100
WEB: http://www.vob.belcarra.bc.ca/

BOWEN ISLAND

Bowen Island offers some of the most beautiful hiking trails found anywhere in B.C. The many lakes, beaches and unspoiled crown forest lands offer residents and visitors a serenity rarely found in the world.

Over 3,000 full time residents call Bowen Island home. In the summer the numbers swell by 50%.

Bowen Island is an enchanting, forested retreat. The island is a delightful 15 minute ferry ride from West Vancouver's Horseshoe Bay.

· 2001 Population: 2,957

CONTACT INFORMATION

· Bowen Island Municipal Council
981 Artisan Lane, Bowen Island, B.C., VON 1G0
Telephone: 604-947-4255
WEB: http://www.bowen-island-bc.com/

BURNABY

Situated on the Burrard Peninsula, between Vancouver to the west and New Westminster and Coquitlam to the east, Burnaby's elevation ranges from sea level to a maximum of 400 metres (1200 feet) atop Burnaby Mountain. Natural features include two large freshwater lakes, naturally forested parkland and a beach on the ocean. A multitude of neighbourhood parks and open spaces provide one with an opportunity to live a lifestyle that includes easy access to physical fitness.

Burnaby offers a full range of housing from single-family to high rise condominiums. The downtown core, Metrotown provides a central and dynamic focus for office, retail, entertainment and hotel accommodation. Burnaby's quality education facilities, including Simon Fraser University and the British Columbia Institute of Technology (BCIT), attract students from across Canada.

Burnaby is centrally located and easily accessed by car, public transit (including SkyTrain) and air via the Vancouver International Airport which is located approximately 20 minutes from the city centre.

• 2001 Population: 193,954

CONTACT INFORMATION

• City of Burnaby
4949 Canada Way, Burnaby, B.C., V5G 1M2
Telephone: 604-294-7944
WEB: http://www.city.burnaby.bc.ca/

CITY OF COQUITLAM

The name Coquitlam is derived from a Salish word meaning small red salmon.

Coquitlam is strategically located at the geographic centre of the Lower Mainland. This makes the city an attractive place for residents, industries and a thriving retail sector. While experiencing rapid growth, Coquitlam has sought to achieve a balance by developing appealing neighbourhoods and vital commercial and industrial areas supported by parks and green space and essential services.

Population trends in Coquitlam are indicative of changes in the region. Greater Vancouver is one of the most rapidly growing areas in Canada, and Coquitlam is among the fastest growing municipalities in the region.

The Westwood lands are located north of the Town Centre. This residential development of cluster homes, townhomes and single family homes has two golf courses, walking trails and gurgling creeks.

Northeast Coquitlam is highlighted by both Minnekhada Regional Park and the southern portion of the massive Pinecone Burke Provincial Park. The 4,000 residents co-exist in a compatible mix of older, well established homes and new neighbourhoods, as well as extensive rural properties and farms.

• 2001 Population: 112,890

CONTACT INFORMATION

• City of Coquitlam
3000 Guildford Way, Coquitlam, B.C., V3B 7N2
Telephone: 604-927-3000
WEB: http://www.city.coquitlam.bc.ca/

THE CORPORATION OF DELTA

Tsawwassen, Ladner and North Delta form the corporation of Delta. These three communities are rich in soil and water, history and industry and especially rich in people.

The residents of these communities are justly proud of the amenities that are vital to the quality of life they enjoy; most obvious is the well-preserved sense of rural living in Delta.

B.C. Ferries run frequent daily service from Tsawwassen Terminal in South Delta to Swartz Bay and Nanaimo (Vancouver Island), the Gulf Islands and Prince Rupert.

• 2001 Population: 96,950

CONTACT INFORMATION

• Municipal Hall
4500 Clarence Taylor Crescent, Delta, B.C. V4K 3E2
Telephone: 604-946-4141
WEB: http://www.corp.delta.bc.ca/

NORTH DELTA

North Delta is the largest residential area in the municipality. Sunshine Hills is a prestigious development with its own tennis court and playground.

2001 Population: 49,500

LADNER

Single family housing still predominates Ladner, which is an older established charming small town. One will also find apartments and townhomes in this community. Delta's municipal centre is located in Ladner and contains the new Municipal Hall, a health centre, the justice building, a transit exchange, an ice arena and a swimming pool.

2001 Population: 21,800

TSAWWASSEN

Tsawwassen is an area whose residents live in prestigious single family dwellings. Higher density housing is limited to low-rise townhomes and apartments.

• 2001 Population: 22,000

CITY OF LANGLEY

The city of Langley consists of established residential neighbourhoods, high density residential development, a revitalized pedestrian oriented downtown and a regional shopping centre. Langley is also one of the most active industrial and service commercial land bases found in the Fraser Valley and Lower Mainland. If you are a nature lover Langley boasts in excess of 300 acres of natural wetland of regional significance.

The City of Langley has managed to retain its small city atmosphere and community spirit while offering all the amenities of a major urban centre. This unique trait appeals to a wide spectrum of people and businesses. It continues to be a community where elected officials are visible neighbours and tax dollars are spent to address local issues.

The city enjoys a temperate climate. The mild winter months average only 10 days of snow per year. This temperate climate helps the area to stay green all year long. Annual precipitation is generally over 1500 mm.

• 2001 Population: 23,643

CONTACT INFORMATION

• City of Langley
20399 Douglas Crescent, Langley, B.C., V3A 4B3
Telephone: 604-514-2800
WEB: http://www.city.langley.bc.ca/

DISTRICT OF MAPLE RIDGE

The district of Maple Ridge is nestled against the Coast Mountains. This is a town that manages to combine small town ambiance with the "busyness" of a major trade centre.

• 2001 Population: 63,169

CONTACT INFORMATION

• District of Maple Ridge
11995 Haney Place, Maple Ridge, B.C., V2X 6A9
Telephone: 604-463-5221
WEB: http://www.district.maple-ridge.bc.ca/

CITY OF NEW WESTMINSTER

New Westminster is located on a hillside overlooking the Fraser River with views of the Golden Ear Mountains.

One can experience excellent views of the Golden Ear Mountains, Mount Baker and the Strait of Georgia from various points within the city. The city is reminiscent of San Francisco with it's sloping streets, waterfront views and heritage buildings.

The city has a strong public sector component, as it is the seat of the New Westminster law courts and the location for the land title office for the lower mainland. Housing styles vary from the large historic homes of Queen's Park to executive style condominiums. A riverfront esplanade provides pedestrian access to a festival market.

With the introduction of SkyTrain connecting New Westminster to Vancouver and Surrey, the City has become the community of choice for many young professional families. The development of the waterfront and the recent commercial and residential development of the former B.C. penitentiary lands, are examples of how B.C.'s original capital city is experiencing a renaissance.

• 2001 Population: 54,656

CONTACT INFORMATION

• City of New Westminster
511 Royal Avenue, New Westminster, B.C., V3L 1H9
Telephone: 604-521-3711
WEB: http://www.city.new-westminster.bc.ca/

CITY OF NORTH VANCOUVER

The city of North Vancouver is a dynamic urban municipality. Eclectic specialty shops abound in this area.

The city offers a diversified economy and wide range of employment, education and recreation opportunities. The establishment of efficient public transportation within the GVRD has contributed to the growing importance of the city of North Vancouver.

The City provides some of the best berthing opportunities on Burrard Inlet. As a result, shipbuilding and the bulk loading of grain, wood products, and other commodities, have provided the City with a strong environmental commitment to develop an attractive community in harmony with nature.

Exceptional recreational amenities provide outdoor enthusiasts an opportunity to sail, swim, hike etc.

The city of North Vancouver enjoys a favourable coastal climate.

· 2001 Population: 44,303

CONTACT INFORMATION

· City of North Vancouver
141 West 14th Street, North Vancouver, B.C., V7M 1H9
Telephone: 604-985-7761
WEB: http://www.cnv.org

DISTRICT OF NORTH VANCOUVER

The District of North Vancouver is the largest of the three North Shore municipalities in both size and population.

The old-fashioned charm of Edgemont with its boutiques, coffee-houses and local restaurants is a popular tourist spot as is nearby Deep Cove. Deep Cove is a small town where mountains and the ocean meet in magnificent beauty. The district has a strong environmental commitment to develop an attractive community in harmony with nature. It would appear that they have been successful thus far.

LOWER CAPILANO

Established as a logging town in the late 19th century, this waterfront port continues to be a major centre of industry. B.C. Rail and Fibreco, the world's largest exporter of chip commodities to the Pacific Rim, have their head offices here.

CAPILANO HIGHLANDS

The areas of Edgemont, Deep Cove and Capilano are main tourist centres.

The Capilano Suspension Bridge, crosses the Capilano River in this Regional Park. Tourists are challenged to cross the bridge which spans 150 metres (450ft) across and 80 metres (230ft) above the river. More than 850,000 visitors cross the bridge each year. Don't worry about the bridge collapsing. It is engineered for complete safety and has the capability of supporting the weight of ten millitary fighter planes.

• 2001 Population: 82,310

CONTACT INFORMATION:

• District of North Vancouver
355 West Queens Road, North Vancouver, B.C., V7N 4N5
Telephone: 604-987-7131
WEB: http://www.district.north-van.bc.ca/

THE DISTRICT OF PITT MEADOWS

Pitt Meadows is considered the "Gateway" to the Fraser Valley. Forty minutes by West Coast Express passenger train and one hour by car from Vancouver's downtown area.

Population growth in Pitt Meadows has generally met or exceeded the B.C. population growth rates in the past ten years. Pitt Meadowss is one of the fastest growing communities in B.C..

Most residents in Pitt Meadows live in an urban town centre area surrounded by agricultural land.

• 2001 Population: 14,670

CONTACT INFORMATION:

• District of Pitt Meadows Municipal Hall
12007 Harris Road, Pitt Meadows, B.C., V3Y 2B5
Telephone: 604-465-5454
WEB: http://www.pittmeadows.bc.ca/

CITY OF PORT COQUITLAM

Port Coquitlam offers the qualities of a small town in a metropolitan region. This city offers one of the finest living and recreational environments in British Columbia.

Port Coquitlam is proud of its unique "PoCo Trail" which encompasses most of the city. The trail is used for nature walks, hikes, bike riding, horseback riding and wildlife watching. The PoCo Trail offers excellent access to the three rivers that grace Port Coquitlam's environment: the Fraser, Pitt and Coquitlam Rivers.

Minnekhada Regional Park, which is a short distance from Port Coquitlam, offers kilometres of natural trails. Ideal for hikers and wildlife watchers, this park boasts beautiful views of the mountains to the north as well as an opportunity to go hiking through mountains in the newly established Burke Mountain Regional Park.

• 2001 Population: 51,257

CONTACT INFORMATION:

• City of Port Coquitlam
2580 Shaughnessy Street, Port Coquitlam, B.C., V3C 2A8
Telephone: 604-927-5411
WEB: http://www.city.port-coquitlam.bc.ca/

CITY OF PORT MOODY

Port Moody is a diverse and charming community. The city has historical importance in Canada. The Canadian Pacific Railway first arrived in British Columbia in 1855 at Port Moody. This city is connected by transit to the city of Vancouver.

Port Moody's natural setting, residential and recreational opportunities and proximity to the nearby Simon Fraser University and Douglas College David Lam Campus, serve as magnets to attract a skilled labour force.

· 2001 Population: 23,816

CONTACT INFORMATION:

· City of Port Moody
100 Newport Drive, Port Moody, B.C., V3H 3E1
Telephone: 604-469-4500
WEB: http://www.cityofportmoody.com/

CITY OF RICHMOND

Richmond is a unique island city located close to the downtown core of Vancouver. Richmond is also ideally situated close to the U.S. border. Richmond is comprised of a series of islands in the mouth of the Fraser river. These islands include Sea Island, most of Lulu Island and fifteen smaller islands.

A dynamic city with a unique mix of residential and commercial property, agricultural lands, industrial parks, waterways and natural areas.

Richmond has undergone enormous change over the last several decades, with significant growth in the early 1990's. Today, Richmond is a dynamic, multi-ethnic community. Much of the recent population growth has been from Asian iimmigrants. They now represent approximately one third of Richmond residents. These newcomers have contributed significantly to the growth of the small business and retail sectors and have added to the diversity and vibrancy of the City of Richmond.

• 2001 Population: 164,345

CONTACT INFORMATION:

• City of Richmond
6911 No. 3 Road,Richmond, B.C., V6Y 2C1
Telephone: 604-276-4000
WEB: http://www.city.richmond.bc.ca/

CITY OF SURREY

Surrey is accessible to all major cities in the Lower Mainland of British Columbia. The recent addition of the Skytrain rapid transit line means Vancouver is less than a 35 minute commute via public transit.

Surrey is recognized as one of the fastest growing cities in Canada. Surrey city centre has been touted as the Lower Mainland's downtown for the Fraser Valley.

Surrey has been divided into six distinct town centres or communities. Each of these communities - Whalley, Guildford, Newton, Fleetwood, Cloverdale and South Surrey has its own unique character.

Surrey has pleasant temperatures all year round with little or no snowfall during the winter months, less rainfall than many neighbouring communities and a significant number of sunshine hours. This enables residents the opportunity to fully enjoy a variety of outdoor pursuits.

• 2001 Population: 347,825

CONTACT INFORMATION:

• City of Surrey
14245 - 56th Avenue, Surrey, B.C., V3X 3A2
Telephone: 604-591-4011
WEB: http://www.city.surrey.bc.ca/

DISTRICT OF WEST VANCOUVER

A combination of beautiful scenery and easy access to downtown make this a favourite destination for many people around the world.

West Vancouver has, over time, grown and developed from a sparsely populated cottage community to a "place of excellence" where residents enjoy a high standard of living. West Vancouver boasts one of the highest average family incomes in Canada. Land values and housing prices are also among the highest in the country.

Most residents emigrated from Great Britain and other northern European countries. However, people from all over the world are now making their homes here, resulting in a more diverse community.

• 2001 Population: 41,421

CONTACT INFORMATION

• West Vancouver Municipal Hall
750-17th Street, West Vancouver, B.C., V7V 3T3
Telephone: 604-925-7000
WEB: http://www.westvancouver.net/

WHITE ROCK

This community is clustered around an eight kilometre sandy beach and the warm shallow waters of Semiahmoo Bay. The area is a preferred retirement community.

The waterfront includes a promenade that spans two and a half kilometres and is fully accessible to the disabled and parents with strollers. The heritage pier, train station, large beached "white rock" and colourful sidewalk cafes create a special ambiance throughout the area.

Commercial meets residential along the waterfront. At the Town Centre you will find a number of apartment buildings with retail stores on the ground level. White Rock has a wide selection of housing from single family homes on small lots to estate lots and multiple family homes.

• 2001 Population: 18,250

CONTACT INFORMATION:

• City of White Rock
15322 Buena Vista Avenue
White Rock, B.C., V4B 1Y6
Telephone: 604-541-2100
WEB: http://www.city.whiterock.bc.ca/

CHAPTER 4: VANCOUVER CONNECTIONS

COMMUNITY SERVICES

• Alcoholics Anonymous
3457 Kingsway
Telephone: 604-434-3933 (24 hours)
WEB: http://www3.bc.sympatico.ca/vanaa/

• Ambleside Animal Hospital
Telephone: 604-922-4157

• BC SPCA Head Office
Telephone: 604-681-7271
WEB: http://www.spca.bc.ca/

• Block Watch
Telephone: 604-717-2857
WEB: http://www.city.vancouver.bc.ca/police/blockwatch/

• Childcare, Childcare Coordinator
Telephone: 604-871-6042

• City of Vancouver
Telephone: 604-873-7011
WEB: http://www.city.vancouver.bc.ca/

• Community Care Facilities, General Inquiries
Telephone: 604-736-2866

• Community Centres, Rinks, Pools, General Inquiries
Telephone: 604-257-8400

• District 1 Al-Anon Family Group
Telephone: 604-688-1716
WEB: http://www.angelfire.com/bc2/alanon/

• Emergency, Police/Fire/Ambulance
Telephone: 911

• Family Services of Greater Vancouver
Telephone: 604-731-4951

• Garbage General Inquiries
Telephone: 604-873-7644

• Kate Booth House, Emergency Shelter
Telephone: 604-872-0772
Telephone: 604-872-7774 **(crisis/urgence)**

• Powell Place Emergency Shelter
Telephone: 604-606-0403

• Recycling Hotline, General Inquiries
Telephone: 604-327-7573

• Utilities, General Inquiries
Telephone: 604-873-7644

• Vancouver Area Network of Drug Users
1st Floor - 50 East Hastings St.
Telephone: 604-683-8595
WEB: http://www.vandu.org/

• Vancouver Fire & Rescue Services
General Inquiries
Telephone: 604-665-6000
WEB: http://www.city.vancouver.bc.ca/fire/

• Vancouver Police
non emergency,
Telephone: 604-665-3535
WEB: http://www.city.vancouver.bc.ca/police/

• Water Rates
Telephone: 604-873-7633

• YMCA
200 - 1166 Alberni Street
Telephone: 604-681-9622
WEB: http://www.ymca.vancouver.bc.ca/

CHILD CARE & DAY CARE

There is a "Child Care Resource and Referral Program" in British Columbia for referrals to child care programs in your community. This program is funded by the Ministry of Children and Families and your municipality. Call Enquiry B.C. 604-660-2421 to get the number of the agency in your area for referral information.

• Acorn Daycare Centre
1525 Taylor Way, West Vancouver
Telephone: 604-922-2933

• Blueridge Preschool
2691 Carnation Street, Deep Cove
Telephone: 604-929-7762

• Bonnie Bairns Child Care Services
2260 Philip, North Vancouver
Telephone: 604-983-2600

• Creekview Tiny Tot Society
1483 Lamey's Mill. Vancouver
Telephone: 604-732-3616

• Dinosaur Daycare
605 Mountain Highway, North Vancouver
Telephone: 604-929-5799
WEB: http://dinosaurdaycare.com/

• Echelon Day Care Centre
575 W 8th. Vancouver
Telephone: 604-874-4010

• Gleneagle Daycare
6404 Wellington Ave., West Vancouver
Telephone: 604-921-9970

• Hudson Out-Of-School Care Society
1551 Cypress St. Vancouver
Telephone: 604-731-1618

• Little Orchard Daycare Ltd.
2707 Violet Street, Deep Cove
Telephone: 604-929-9692

• Milestone Montessori Pre-School & Kindergarten
9316 116th St., Delta
Telephone: 604-583-1446,

• Westcoast Child Care Resource Centre
Third Floor 210 West Broadway
Telephone: 604-709-5661
WEB: http://www.wstcoast.org/

• YMCA Child Care
#500 - 1188 West Georgia St.
Telephone: 604-294-9622
WEB: http://www.ymca.vancouver.bc.ca/

• WestCoast Families, Vancouver's Resource for Family Life!
WEB: http://www.westcoastfamilies.com/html/vancouver.html

• French Preschool in Surrey, B.C. for the 3 to 5 years old.
WEB: http://www.lacoccinelle.org/

• Westcoast Child Care Resource Centre
WEB: http://www.wstcoast.org/

• Children's & Women's Health Centre of British Columbia
4500 Oak Street
Telephone: 604-875-2000
WEB: http://www.cw.bc.ca/

ENTERTAINMENT & ACTIVITIES

Vancouver offers outstanding choices and quality when it comes to dining, arts, culture and entertainment. Being a "melting-pot" of cultural groups, Vancouver has a large variety of restaurants for every taste and budget. Symphony orchestra, Vancouver Opera Company, Vancouver Bach Choir, Vancouver CBC Orchestra, world famous Vancouver Art Gallery, Vancouver Museum and a range of other interesting museums, multicultural attractions, as well as many musical venues, reflect Vancouver's ethnic and cultural diversity.

Vancouver is home to the Celebration of Light, the du Maurier International Jazz Festival, La Quena Latin America Fiesta, Fringe Festival and numerous cultural events.

INFORMATION

• Vancouver Tourist info Centre
Plaza Level, 200 Burrard Street
Telephone: 604-683-2000
WEB: http://www.tourism-vancouver.org/

• Vancouver International Children's Festival
WEB: http://www.vancouverchildrensfestival.com

• HSBC Powersmart Celebration of Light
WEB: http://www.celebration-of-light.com

• Festival Vancouver
WEB: http://www.festivalvancouver.bc.ca

• Vancouver Folk Music Festival
WEB: http://www.thefestival.bc.ca

• Bard on the Beach Shakespeare Festival
WEB: http://www.bardonthebeach.org

• The Vancouver Fringe Festival
WEB: http://www.vancouverfringe.com

CULTURAL STATISTICS				
Museums	Dance Companies	Opera	Symphony	Theatres
56	29	1	7	27

- Cycling BC, 332-1367 West Broadway
Telephone: 604-737-3142

- H.R. MacMillan Planetarium
Telephone: 604-738-7827
WEB: http://www.hrmacmillanspacecentre.com/

- Pacific National Exhibition
Telephone: 604-253-2311
WEB: http://www.pne.bc.ca/

- Science World
Telephone: 604-443-7440
WEB: http://www.scienceworld.bc.ca/

- Vancouver Aquarium Marine Science Centre
Telephone: 604-659-3474
WEB: http://www.vanaqua.org/

- Vancouver Board of Parks and Recreation, 2099 Beach Avenue
Telephone: 604-257-8400

- Vancouver Maritime Museum
Telephone: 604-257-8300
WEB: http://www.vmm.bc.ca/i

- Vancouver Museum
Telephone: 604-736-4431
WEB: http://www.vanmuseum.bc.ca/

- Vancouver Art Gallery
Telephone: 604-662-4719
WEB: http://www.vanartgallery.bc.ca/

- Vancouver Civic Theatres
Telephone: 604-665-3050
WEB: http://www.city.vancouver.bc.ca/theatres/index.html

- Vancouver Opera
Telephone: 604-683-0222
WEB: http://www.vanopera.bc.ca/

- Vancouver Symphony Orchestra
Telephone: 604-684-9100
WEB: http://www.vancouversymphony.ca/

HEALTH

MEDICAL SERVICES PLAN OF BC (MSP)

Enrollment with MSP is voluntary. Residents who want coverage for themselves and their dependants must register with MSP. Under the Medical and Health Care Services Act, a resident is defined as a person makes his or her home in B.C.

Tourists or visitors to B.C do not qualify for coverage.

When enrolling with MSP, photocopies of documents verifying Canadian citizenship or immigration status must accompany registration forms.

HOW TO REGISTER FOR MSP

Application forms can be obtained from MSP or any Government Agent/ BC Access Centre. You will be asked to send copies of documents to support citizenship or the immigration status of the persons listed on your application.

If coverage is available through your employer, union or pension plan, contact their office for information and an application form.

CONTACT INFORMATION:

Telephone: 604-683-7151
WEB: http://www.healthservices.gov.bc.ca/msp/

• Ministry of Health's General Information Line
Telephone: 1-800-465-4911
WEB: http://www.gov.bc.ca/healthservices/

• Vancouver General Hospital
855 W 12th Ave.
Telephone: 604-875-4111
WEB: http://www.vanhosp.bc.ca/

PHARMACARE

Pharmacare is British Columbia's drug insurance program that assists residents with paying for eligible prescription drugs and designated medical supplies.

For hospital inpatients, drugs are an expense of the hospital system. Once the patient is discharged, Pharmacare becomes the responsible agency, within the terms of established eligibility requirements.

INFORMATION

• Pharmacare
Telephone: 604-682-6849
WEB: http://www.healthservices.gov.bc.ca/pharme/

HOSPITAL INSURANCE

Hospital insurance is provided to all eligible residents of BC. It is not necessary to register or pay premiums. There is no charge for acute care, in-patient or out-patient services received in the province. Payment of hospital charges outside Canada will not exceed $75.00 day.

INFORMATION

Telephone: 604-683-7151
WEB: https://bchealthguide.org/

AMBULANCE SERVICE

Ambulance service is subsidized by the Province of British Columbia. There is a user fee for this service. Ambulance service does not provide out-of-province benefits.

INFORMATION

Telephone: 1-800-665-7199
WEB: http://www.healthservices.gov.bc.ca/bcas/

PACIFIC BLUE CROSS

Pacific Blue Cross is British Columbia's largest provider of extended health and dental benefits. The system was created in the 1940's with the inception of two organizations who then merged in 1997 to become Pacific Blue Cross. From small beginnings, Pacific Blue Cross now offers service to more than 2 milion people.

INFORMATION

Telephone: 1-888-275-4672
WEB: http://www.pac.bluecross.ca/

VANCOUVER COASTAL HEALTH AUTHORITY

The Vancouver Coastal Health Authority and the three Health Service Delivery Areas is home to 25 per cent of B.C.'s population. The area includes 12 acute care facilities and two diagnostic treatment centres. The area has just over 7,000 residential care beds.

INFORMATION

• Vancouver Coastal Health Authority
 #200 - 520 West 6th Avenue, Vancouver, B.C., V5Z 4H5
Telephone: 604-736-033
WEB: http://www.vancoastalhealth.ca/

LEISURE AND RECREATION

Every municipality/district in the Greater Vancouver Area has a parks and recreation department. Community centres in and around the area offer programs such as swimming, skating, fitness classes, dance lessons, teen drop in centres and seniors programs. Most community centres are well used and well maintained. The programs are reasonably priced.

Community centres can be a great way to meet people when you are new to the city. If you are a parent with children at home and you do not go out to work, the parks and recreation department offers many programs geared toward stay at home parents. They offer programs such as mom/dad and child artist, mom/dad and child music and mom/dad and child swimming.

• City of Vancouver Parks & Recreation
WEB: http://www.city.vancouver.bc.ca/parks/

• GVRD Parks
Telephone: 604-432-6200
WEB: http://www.gvrd.bc.ca/

VANCOUVER YEARLY EVENTS

• Cloverdale Rodeo & Exhibition: May

• International Jazz Festival: June

• Pacific National Exhibition: August

• Symphony of Fire (Fireworks Competition):   July-August

• Vancouver International Children's Festival: May-June

• Vancouver International Film Festival: September-October

VANCOUVER PUBLIC LIBRARY

Vancouver Public Library is the second largest public library system in Canada, with over 395,000 cardholders and more than 8 million items borrowed annually. The Vancouver Public Library system has 20 branches throughout GVRD.

You can borrow
• books
• videotapes
• DVDs
• CD's
• music tapes,
• magazines
and more if you have a library card.

The library is also an excellent resource for compiling research for students, gathering information for small business owners. Material can be found in many languages.

If you wish to use the public libraries you must apply for a library card.

Library cards are free to:
• all people who live in the City of Vancouver.
• all people who own property in the City of Vancouver.
• all people who live within the region served by the public
• libraries who are part of the **Public Library InterLINK.**

(Interlink is a partnership of strong local libraries which promotes the provision of quality library services to residents through open access to member libraries.)

If you do not qualify for a card under these guidelines, you must pay a minimal non-resident fee. This will enable you to receive either a visitor's card or a subscription card with full library privileges.

WEB: http://www.bcpl.gov.bc.ca/interlink/

GVRD LIBRARY BRANCHES

• City of Vancouver Central Library
350 West Georgia
Telephone: 604-331-3603
WEB: http://www.vpl.vancouver.bc.ca/

• Burnaby Public Library
4595 Albert St., Burnaby
Telephone: 604-299-8955
WEB: http://www.bpl.burnaby.bc.ca/

• Coquitlam Public Library
3001 Burlington Drive Coquitlam
Telephone: 604- 927-3560
WEB: http://www.library.coquitlam.bc.ca/

• New Westminster Public Library
716 6th Ave.New Westminster,
Telephone: 604-527-4660
WEB: http://www.nwpl.new-westminster.bc.ca/

• North Vancouver City Library
121 West 14th Street
Telephone: 604-998-3490
WEB: http://www.cnv.org/nvcl/

• Richmond Public Library
100-7700 Minoru Gate
Telephone: 604-231-6405
WEB: http://www.rpl.richmond.bc.ca/

• University of British Columbia Library
1958 Main Mall, Vancouver
Telephone: 604-822-6375
WEB: http://www.library.ubc.ca/

• West Vancouver Memorial Library
1950 Marine Drive
Telephone: 604-925-7400
WEB: http://www.westvanlib.org/

NEWCOMERS CLUB OF B.C.

The newcomers association is a great resource. Concerns about area orientation, clubs, sport groups, transit questions and school issues can all be addressed through a newcomers club.

It is also a great way to make acquaintances in your new area.

The following web site will provide you with more information on the many associations in the Vancouver area.

WEB: http://www.newcomersclub.com/bc.html

WELCOME WAGON

Welcome Wagon is a service provided by local community businesses. A representative will present you with an information package including local phone numbers, free samples of various items and maps.

WEB: http://www.welcomewagon.ca/

DID YOU KNOW

That the North Shore Mountains have played the role of "backdrop" in quite a few movies including, The Changeling, Crackerjack, Narrow Margin, Roxanne, and Russian Roulette, and TV series episodes from Cobra, The Fall Guy, MacGyver, The Outer Limits, and The X-Files.

PLACES OF WORSHIP

Canada is a country of democratic freedoms for all people. As a Canadian one has the right to practise their religion without fear of prosection. This tolerant policy has provided many religious communities an opportunity to worship in their own faith.

• Anglican Church Diocese, 401 W. Georgia
Telephone: 604-684-5306

• Augustana Lutheran Church, 5 W. King Edward
Telephone: 604- 876-7814

• Archdiocese of Vancouver, 150 Robson Street
Telephone: 604-683-0281

• British Columbia Muslim Association
12300 Blundell, Richmond
Telephone: 604-270-2522

• Christ The Redeemer, 599 Keith Road
Telephone: 604-922-1371

• Congregation Beth Israel 4350 Oak Street
Telephone: 604-731-4161

• Holy Rosary Cathedral, 646 Richards St.
Telephone: 604-682-6774

• Islamic Information Centre
3127 Kingsway, Vancouver
Telephone: 604-434-7526

• Korean United Church Of Canada
2855 E. 1st, Vancouver
Telephone: 604-255-7002

• Nanaksar Gurdwara Gursikh Temple
18691 Westminster Highway Richmond
Telephone: 604-270-7369

GVRD RELIGIOUS INSTITUTIONS			
Protestant	Catholic	Synagogues	Other
769	85	13	124

- United Church BC
4383 Rumble Street Burnaby,
Telephone: 604-431-0434

- Vancouver Buddhist Church
220 Jackson St.
Telephone: 604-253-7033

- Vancouver Chinese Lutheran Church
1005 Kensington Avenue, Burnaby
Telephone: 604-299-4977

- Vietnamese Alliance Church
7155 Sherbrooke St.
Telephone: 604-321-7868

- World Harvest Church
7451 Elmbridge Way
Telephone: 604-271-4250

PROFESSIONAL ASSOCIATIONS

- Association of B.C. Professional Foresters (ABCPF)
Suite 1201, 1130 West Pender Street, B.C., V6E 4A4
Telephone: 604-687-8027
WEB: http://www.rpf-bc.org/

- Association of Professional Engineers and Geoscientists of B.C.
200 - 4010 Regent Street, Burnaby, B.C., V5C 6N2
Telephone: 604-430-8035
WEB: http://www.apeg.bc.ca/

- British Columbia Teachers' Federation
100–550 West 6th Avenue Vancouver, B.C., V5Z 4P2
Telephone: 604-871-2283
WEB: http://www.bctf.ca/

- Canadian Home Builders' Association
3700 Willingdon Avenue Burnaby, B..C, V5G 3H2
Telephone: 604-432-7112
WEB: http://www.chbabc.org/

• Hong Kong Canada Business Association
885 Georgia St W, Vancouver
Telephone: 604-684-2410
WEB: http://www.hkcba.com/

• National Association of Asian American Professionals
Kingsway R.P.O. PO Box 79018, Vancouver, B.C., V5R 5Z6
Telephone: 604-515-5771
WEB: http://www.naaap.bc.ca/

• Registered Nurses' Association of British Columbia
2855 Arbutus Street Vancouver, B.C., V6J 3Y8
Telephone: 604-736-7331
WEB: http://www.rnabc.bc.ca/

• The Coaches Association of BC
345-1367 West Broadway, Vancouver, B.C., V6H 4A9
Telephone: 604-298-3137
WEB: http://www.coaches.bc.ca/

DID YOU KNOW

That Canada Place was built to coincide with Expo 86
when it was used to house the government of
Canada's pavilion, Canada Place sits at the foot of
Howe Street, extending into the harbour. Resembling
a giant cruise ship, Canada Place has become a
major Vancouver landmark. It's home to the Vancouver
Trade and Convention Centre, a cruise-ship terminal,
The Prow Restaurant, the Pan Pacific Hotel, a selection
of retail shops, a food court and the CN IMAX Theatre.

SPORTS

It has been said that in Vancouver, one can ski in the morning, golf in the afternoon and enjoy peaceful sailing in the evening.

The world renowned ski resorts, Whistler and Blackcomb, are only 90 minutes north of Vancouver. Vancouver boasts numerous golf courses, tennis clubs, yacht clubs, marinas, ski hills & other recreational facilities.

A mild climate offers cyclists the opportunity to enjoy recreational riding as well as an alternative mode of transportation. Sailing, hockey, lacrosse, kayaking, fishing and canoeing are among the choices for the sports enthusiast.

• B.C. Open Water Swim Association
Telephone: 604-290-9425
WEB: http://vowsa.bc.ca

• B.C. Place Stadium, 777 Pacific Blvd.
Telephone: 604-669-2300
WEB: http://www.bcpavco.com/bcplacestadium/

• General Motors Place
(Home of the Vancouver Canucks)
800 Griffiths Way Vancouver, B.C., V6B 6G1
Telephone: 604-899-7400
WEB: http://www.canucks.com/gm/

• Grouse Mountain Resorts Ltd.
6400 Nancy Greene Way North Vancouver, B.C., V7R 4K9
Telephone: 604-984-0661
WEB: http://www.grousemtn.com/

• Morgan Creek Golf Course
3500 Morgan Creek Way, South Surrey, B.C., V3S 0J7
Telephone: 604-531-4653
WEB: http://www.morgancreekgolf.com/

• Pacific Coast Amateur Hockey Association
Unit # 114 - 3993 Henning Drive, Burnaby, B.C.
Telephone: 604-205-9011
WEB: http://www.pcaha.bc.ca

• Sport BC
409 - 1367 West Broadway Vancouver, B.C., V6H 4A9
Telephone: Membership Directory 604-737-3000
WEB: http://www.sport.bc.ca/

• The BC Lions Football Club
Telephone: 604-930-5466
WEB: http://www.bclions.com/

• The Stanley Park Ecology Society
Telephone: 604-257-6908
WEB: http://www.vcn.bc.ca/spes/

• Vancouver Bicycle Club
Telephone: 604-733-3964
WEB: http://vbc.bc.ca/

• Vancouver Canucks Ice Hockey Team
Telephone: 604-899-7400
WEB: http://www.canucks.com/

• Vancouver Curling Club
Telephone: 604-874-0122
WEB: http://www.vancouvercurlingclub.com/

• Whistler Blackcomb Mountains
Telephone: 604-932-3434
WEB: http://www.blackcomb.com/

The Pacific dogwood was adopted in 1956 as
British Columbia's floral emblem. The Pacific dogwood is
a tree that grows six to eight metres high and flowers in
April and May. In the autumn it is conspicuous for its
cluster of bright red berries and brilliant foliage.

UTILITIES

> If you are phoning from Vancouver you have to dial
> 10 digits for every phone call. Dial 604 and then the
> 7 digit telephone number.

B.C. Gas is the largest distributor of natural gas in British Columbia. Their gas distribution business serves 762,000 customers in more than 100 communities.

• B.C. Gas Utility Ltd.
16705 Fraser Highway Surrey, B.C., V3S 2X7
Telephone: 1-800-561-442
WEB: http://www.bcgas.com/

• B.C. Hydro information and application for new service
Telephone: 1-800-224-9376
WEB: https://eww.bchydro.bc.ca/customerservice/apply.html

• B.C. Hydro, Power Smart Information
Telephone: 1-877-431-9463
WEB: https://eww.bchydro.bc.ca/powersmart/

• Shaw Cable, 1600-4710 Kingsway, Burnaby, B.C., V5H 4M5
Telephone: 604-629-8888
WEB: http://shaw.ca/

• Telus, (B.C.'s Phone Company) Customer Service:
Business Telephone Information, **Telephone:** 604-310-3100

Residential Telephone Information, **Telephone:** 604-310-2255
WEB: http://www.telus.com/

CHEAP ELECTRICITY

Did you know that British Columbians enjoy some of the lowest electricity prices in the world? Residential power is cheaper here than in Toronto, Calgary, Seattle and Los Angeles.

POSTAL SERVICE

Canada Post Corporation (CPC) and its affiliate, Purolator Courier Ltd. collected, processed, and delivered 9.61 billion pieces of mail and parcels during the 1998-1999 fiscal year.

Canada Post collects, processes, and delivers mail across the world's second-largest country (second in geographical size only to Russia).

Each working day, CPC and its affiliate deliver an average of 38 million pieces of mail, processed through 22 major plants and many other facilities, to over 12.9 million addresses in Canada, and forwards mail to virtually every country in the world.

Canada Post offers customers a network of 18,600 retail points of access. 78% of these locations are operated by private businesses.

In August 1999 the Government of Canada approved a series of proposals to enhance the range and access of retail postal services in rural Canada, allowing better access for these communities.

The cost of mailing a letter anywhere in Canada is currently 48 cents.

Canada Post:

General Information, **Telephone: 1 800 267-1177**

From outside of Canada, **Telephone: 1 416 979-8822**

WEB: http://www.postescanada.ca/

VOLUNTEERING

Keep in mind that if you are moving with a partner or family, they may feel quite isolated at this time. It is important that they be introduced to the newcomers club or similar club in your area. Perhaps volunteer work is the answer to the inevitable loneliness or an opportunity to return to academic upgrading. You may not have the same feeling of alienation because you will have your work to keep you occupied but be prepared for some negative feedback from your partner/spouse.

Volunteer work provides a sense of pride, accomplishment, work experience and as well as an opportunity to become acquainted with people from the area.

We have included a partial list of contacts for volunteering opportunities. Consult the yellow pages for a more concise list.

• Delta Family and Community Services
Telephone: 604-946-2042
WEB: http://www.deltassist.com

• Greater Coquitlam Volunteer Centre
Telephone: 604-524-9808
WEB: http://www.volunteercentre.org

• Greater Vancouver Food Bank Society
Telephone: 604-876-3601
WEB: http://www.foodbank.bc.ca/

• North Shore Community Services
Telephone: 604-985-7168
WEB: http://www.vcn.bc.ca/nscs

· Richmond Connections Information and Volunteer Society
Telephone: 604-278-5244
WEB: http://www.vcn.bc.ca/rcs

· Surrey Community Volunteer Services
Telephone: 604-584-5811

· United Way of the Lower Mainland
4543 Canada Way, Burnaby
Telephone: 604-294-8929
WEB: http://www.uwlm.ca/

· Vancouver Volunteer Centre
#301 - 3102 Main Street
Telephone: 604-875-9144
WEB: http://www.vancouver.volunteer.ca/

· Volunteer BC
Telephone: 604-875-9144
WEB: http://www.volunteerbc.bc.ca

· Volunteer Burnaby
Telephone: 604-294-5533
WEB: http:// www.volunteerburnaby.ca

· White Rock - Peace Arch Community Services
Telephone: 250-531-6226
WEB: http://www.pacsbc.com

VOLUNTEERING

Volunteering is a useful tool for work experience.
It will be easier to present yourself to prospective
employers if you have shown an interest in your
community through volunteering.

STATISTICAL INFORMATION

We live in a moving world and instead of showing tables with prices and other stats that will be outdated within 6 months, we decided to give you information on where to find the most "Up to Date" information available.

GREATER VANCOUVER HOUSE PRICES

The Real Estate Weekly is the source for Real Estate information, with 16 publications delivered to over 500,000 homes and Real Estate offices throughout the Lower Mainland each week.

WEB Statistics: http://rew.bc.ca/stats.htm

BC STATS

Located in Victoria, British Columbia, Canada, BC Stats is the central statistical agency of the Province of British Columbia. They have the provincial government's largest concentration of statistical products, services and expertise.

• BC Statistics
Box 9410 Stn Prov Govt Victoria, B.C., V8W 9V1
Telephone: 250- 387-0327
WEB Statistics: http://www.bcstats.gov.bc.ca/

Quick Facts about British Columbia a ready reference for anyone seeking a comprehensive picture of British Columbia. You will find descriptions of British Columbia's economic and geographic diversity, its social priorities, recreation facilities and its standing within Canada.

WEB Statistics: http://www.bcstats.gov.bc.ca/data/qf.pdf

MINISTRY OF EDUCATION STATISTICS

The BC Ministry of Education maintains Statistics on a variety of subjects such as "School Lists and Organization Reports", "Grade Enrolment Reports ", "Course Enrolment/Class Size Reports " covering the Greater Vancouver area and the rest of B.C..

WEB Statistics: http://www.bced.gov.bc.ca/k12datareports/

STATISTICS CANADA

Statistics Canada has a wealth of information for anybody looking for statistical information on Greater Vancouver and the rest of Canada.

Statistics Canada Advisory Services
600-300 West Georgia Street, Vancouver, B.C., V6B 6C7
Telephone: 604-666-3691
WEB Statistics: http://www.statcan.ca/

OTHER STATISTICAL INFORMATION

Statistical information about the Greater Vancouver Area can also be found here:

WEB: http://relocatecanada.com/statisticshelper.html

WEB: http://relocatecanada.com/stathousehold.html

WEB: http://relocatecanada.com/incomestats.html

VANCOUVER STATISTICS
Household Income Distribution

Under - $ 53,000	54.1 %
$53,000- $77,000	18.5 %
$77,000- $115,000	17.2 %
$115,00 - Above	10.2 %

COMMUNITY QUESTIONS

Some questions you should ask when you are planning your relocation/ move.

COMMUNITY

- Is the area urban, suburban or rural.
- What kind of town, satelite, historic, resort or company.
- Housing density.
- Area zoning.
- Does the community have the housing style you will be seeking.
- Is the community's population growing, declining, stable mobile.
- What is the average income.
- What is the structure and reputation of local government.
- Does the community have its own economic base.
- What is the extent of industrial and commercial development.

TRANSPORTATION

- Is public transportation available.
- What are monthly commuting costs.
- How many kilometres to work.
- Travel time ?

SHOPPING

- as part of the central business district.
- in major shopping centres.
- through neighbourhood stores and services.

HEALTH

- local doctors, dentists and other health professonals.
- hospital(s) clinics/medical centres/health clubs.

MUNICIPAL SERVICES AND RESOURCES

- cable, antenna.
- electricity/garbage collection.
- gas/sewer/water/snow removal/public library.
- active public recreation (parks, playgrounds).
- recreation centre/swimming pool.

CULTURE AND ENTERTAINMENT

- music/theatre (live/films)/museums.
- sports arenas/nightlife.
- cable, antenna.

EDUCATION

- elementary, secondary, community college.
- special education.
- vocational/technical.
- post-graduate (type) universities.

RELIGION

Is a church/synagogue/house of worship of your choice available?

RECREATIONAL/SPORTS ACTIVITIES

- baseball, YMCA/YWCA.
- community centre.
- hockey, public swimming.
- country club, public golf course.
- health club, public tennis courts.
- soccer, riding stables.
- football.
- parks, outdoor activities.

CHAPTER 5: HOUSING

HOUSING STYLES

RESIDENTIAL HOMES

There are many different styles of houses. Real estate listings will include such terms as bungalow, detached and townhome. We have included some here.

- bungalow: all rooms are on one level, plus a basement.
- 2 storey: rooms on two levels, plus a basement.
- detached: not attached to any other houses. Free standing.
- semi-detached: attached to another house, on one side.
- townhouse: several houses attached in a row.
- condominium: detached, maintenance free apartment.
  (the unit itself is owned by a person but the property is maintained by service personnel hired by the condominium corporation. Strata Corporation in B.C.).
- link home: attached to another house underground.
- ranch bungalow: sprawling bungalow.
- single family dwelling: suitable for one family.

A house with a garage is either listed as "attached garage" or "detached garage." An attached garage means the garage is actually part of the house structure with an entrance directly into the house. A detached garage means the garage is separate from the house and probably does not provide direct access to the house.

Some people consider the basement area to be extra living space and design this part of the house with that in mind.

HOUSING STYLES
RENTAL PROPERTIES

Terms that you may come across while searching for your rental property may be unfamiliar to you. We have listed some rental terms here to help ease the confusion.

- bachelor apartment: one large living area, separate kitchen, bathroom.

- studio apartment: one large living area including kitchen, bathroom.

- one bedroom: living area, kitchen, bathroom, bedroom.

- two bedroom: living area, kitchen, bathroom, 2 bdrm.   .

- three bedroom: living area, kitchen, bathroom, 3 bdrm.

- loft: warehouse space converted into living space.

- basement apartment: lower level of a house.

- duplex, two houses built together.

These terms are also relevant to condominium buildings.

- A condominium building is a high rise complex similar to an apartment building but each unit is owned, not rented.

- Most apartment buildings offer some amenities, and laundry is usually done in a central area such as a laundry room in the basement.

HOUSING TERMS

FYI

Real estate listings may differ as well. There are several terms used by real estate agents that a new home owner/renter probably would not recognize, for example elf, cac and eac. Here are some more examples; try to guess the answers.

elf, tba, fag, ftcobfp, agdo, eac, pta, uffi, ss

Okay, how did you do? If you scored 8 or more you should forget the relocation offer and go to work as a real estate agent. If you scored 5-8 you probably live in Vancouver already or you know someone who does.

If you scored less than 5 you are in good company.

Here are the definitions of the acronyms.

elf: Not little people residing on the premises, this term refers to electric light fixtures. This is included in virtually all listings because, believe it or not, some vendors have been known to take the light fixtures with them, even those tacky globe lights found in many a hallway. There are exceptions to this clause and they will be noted on the listing. For example, if a person has installed a chandelier, tiffany style light or any other lighting that they want to take with them when they move, the listing may read as follows, under the listing for chattels: "all elfs on premises included, with the exclusion of chandelier in main level foyer." This makes it very clear that the chandelier is NOT to be included in the items being left in the house by the vendor.

fag: Not a politically incorrect name for cigarettes or anything else, the term is an acronym for forced air gas, which is the principle source of heating in most homes. Some houses are heated with oil, electric heat or water radiators, but gas remains the first choice for energy efficiency.

eac: Not a men's aftershave, this term is an acronym for electronic air cleaners. With allergies becoming more and more common many homeowners have begun installing electronic air cleaners in their homes.

uffi: Not an exotic pet or cutesy name for a pet, this term is an acronym for urea formaldehyde foam insulation. In the early 1970s the housing industry began installing uffi as an alternative insulation source from the fibreglass insulation they had been using. The Canadian government even offered homeowners grants to install the uffi in order to encourage energy conservation. Unfortunately many people became ill from the fumes that emanated from the uffi and eventually, all homes that contained any uffi had to have all of it removed.

It is illegal to have uffi in a home or to build a home using uffi. It is also mandatory, if uffi is present in a home, that the agent disclose such information. This should be included somewhere on a real estate listing.

ss: Not a division of the German army, this term is an acronym for storms and screens, referring to the doors and windows. Some houses have a second door on the outside of the house which is called a storm door and many houses have screens installed on their outside windows, hence the term storms and screens.

tba: An acronym for "to be arranged". This term is usually used in the context of arranging dates for moving in or out, for example the listing may read "Possession date January 1, 2002 or tba." The vendor is showing some flexibility in the possession date and stating that this is a negotiable item.

ftcobfp: Not a profanity in another language, this term is an acronym for floor to ceiling, open brick fireplace.

agdo: Not a new group on the music scene, this term is an acronym for automatic garage door opener. This is a fairly new item on real estate listings since many homes did not have automatic garage door openers until recently. It is fairly common practice to have them installed automatically in newer homes and many owners of older homes are finding the convenience of an automatic garage door opener worthy of the expense as well.

pta: Not a term referring to education/school committees, this term is an acronym for purchaser to arrange. The term usually refers to mortgage arrangements. The vendor may choose to keep their mortgage and transfer it to their new property or to property or to discharge it completely. In this case the purchaser is responsible to arrange a mortgage on the property. The real estate agent can provide the purchaser with the pertinent information or names and numbers of somebody who can be of assistance. All financial institutions offer mortgage assistance if you qualify.

The Steller's jay became BC's official bird on December 17, 1987. Coloured a vibrant blue and black, it is found throughout the province. This lively, smart and cheeky bird was voted most popular bird by the people of British Columbia.

PURCHASING A HOME OR CONDOMINIUM

If you are buying or renting a property ask your human resources representative at your new placement if he/she has a working relationahip with a real estate agency or relocation firm.This is an advantage when starting a home search.

You may have the option of working with an assigned agent or deciding to choose an agent of your own. It is always best to work with somebody who is familiar with corporate relocations and can explain the home buying/renting process.

There are many differences between American and Canadian house buying procedures.The main difference, and perhaps the most surprising to Americans, is the non-deductible mortgage payment in Canada.

Homeowners in the U.S. may deduct their mortgage interest payments from their taxable income. This is NOT the case in Canada. Canadians CANNOT deduct their mortgage interest payments from their taxable income.

Mortgage terms are different. In the United States a mortgage is set up with a pre-determined ammortization period, for example 25 years. The interest rate and mortgage payments remain the same for 25 years. In Canada, the mortgage is set up with a pre-determined ammortization period, for example 25 years, but the interest rate is renegotiated during this time period.

LEAKS

Vancouver is a region that receives more precipitation than many other cities. This has caused problems in the commercial construction industry. Many condominium owners (aproximately 50%) have had to bare the burden of having the exterior of their units repaired or replaced due to extensive water damage.

The problem became a provincial issue in the early 1990s as so many homeowners were affected by the damage and insurance would not cover the cost of repairs.
The government intervened and strict building codes have been set in place in an effort to ammend the problem.

This means that a mortgage holder has to renegotiate the terms of the mortgage several times as specified by the financial contract. For example, the Smiths have a $50,000.00 mortgage on their home. The interest rate has been set at 7%, paid annually, for an ammortization period of 25 years, but renewable in 5 years. In five years the Smith's will have paid off some of the mortgage principal but the remainder will have to be renegotiated at the current interest rates. This creates uncertainty for many homeowners who cannot predict the trend of interest rates.

Many people got caught in a financial web in the mid 1980's. Homeowners had mortgages coming up for renewal and interest rates were at an all time high of 21%! For many people this rise in monthly mortgage payments meant financial ruin and houses were repossessed. There were no alternatives...one could pay the hike in the interest rate, which had climbed from 10% to 21% in less than 2 years, or pay a penalty to renegotiate the mortgage rate at a lower rate. If one chose to renegotiate the rate a loss of income had to be paid to the mortgage broker by the homeowner....it was a lose, lose situation.

HOME PURCHASING OPTIONS

The internet has changed the way many real estate companies market their properties. A prospective buyer can search the internet, find something suitable, take a virtual tour of the property, receive information concerning the general area, ask questions about the property and even make an offer!

An alternative to using the services of a real estate agent is to visit new home building sites. This option is for new home construction only. A prospective home buyer can go to the site, preview the house plans and community development plans and tour through the model homes. Builders have model homes to feature their products. Walking through a model home provides more clarity and encourages questions from prospective buyers. Carpet colours, ceramic tiles, size and shape of windows, room layout, counter tops, color and materials can all be previewed in a model home.

A further option for home purchase is a private sale. A vendor will market their home for sale through a series of venues: the internet, local newspaper advertising, putting a sign on the lawn, contacting people who may have shown an interest in the property in the past,through co-workers. People sell privately to save the commission fee payable to real estate agents for doing the same thing. Selling privately can work but it is tricky.

A vendor really has to know the real estate market and a prospective purchaser has to really know what to watch out for. Make yourself knowledgeable about the area, the price of homes recently sold that are comparable to the ones you are looking at, don't sign any contracts or paperwork until a real estate lawyer has previewed them, don't leave any deposits with the purchaser until a lawyer has approved the contracts. Your signature on a document is legal and makes a contract a binding agreement.

Take your time, think things through and don't be pressured into making any quick decisions.

ROLE OF A REAL ESTATE AGENT

You have picked a home you like. It has taken much looking but it was worth the effort. Now your work is done, at least for a little while.

A realtor is indispensable during the sometimes stressful negotiation period. They have been through this process many times and understand the finer points of offers and counter offers

• prepare an offer to purchase the property
• advise on negotiations and terms of contract
• present the offer to the vendors
• negotiate the contract on behalf of the purchaser
• represent your best interests during negotiations
• assist in preparations of contracts, explain any conditions
• collect down payments.

An offer to purchase is prepared by your real estate agent not the vendor's agent. It will include details on the price you are prepared to pay for the property, the date you want to take possession of the property, any appliances that you do or do not want left with the property and the amount of the deposit. This is a standard offer. It should include a request for a disclosure statement from the vendor indicating that, to his/her knowledge, there are no serious issues concerning house deterioration such as house rot. This clause does not preclude any requests by the purchaser that a home inspection be done.

A date and time of acceptance is written into the contract and, if specific terms and conditions have not been agreed to by this time, the contract becomes null and void. This is what the industry calls a "conditional sale." In this situation the house is put back on the market.

When the offer is accepted by the purchaser and the vendor this becomes a binding agreement.

MORTGAGE TRIVIA

In the word mortgage, the mort- is from the Latin word for death and -gage is from the sense of that word meaning a pledge to forfeit something of value if a debt is not repaid. So mortgage is literally a dead pledge. It was dead for two reasons, the property was forfeit or "dead" to the borrower if the loan was not repaid and the pledge itself was dead if the loan was repaid.
The word is 14th century in origin.

WHAT TO WATCH FOR

- know exactly what you are signing. Your signature on a contract is a legal document.
- request a home inspection prior to move in date. Include this request on the offer to purchase with a clause indicating that if there is a serious structural flaw with the property you are not responsible for taking possession of the property.
- don't be pressured into signing documents. Buying a home is stressful,
- be very clear about what you are signing.
- work with a reputable real estate agent. Ask people to recommend agents and their reasons for the recommendation.
- take your time house hunting. Know what you want and remain focused on those wants.
- be realistic about your price range. Don't look at properties that are beyond your budget.
- know the neighbourhood.
- are there any trains, airports or other noisy distractions nearby?
- deposits are made out to the real estate company, in trust, and held by the company until closing date. No other fees should be paid out.
- a vendor pays real estate commission fees, not a purchaser.

MORTGAGES

Any Mortgage term 3 years or longer is considered "long term" in today's economy. Because long-term rates are usually higher than short-term rates, you may not want to choose this option. On the other hand, by locking in you will avoid exposure to rate increases. You'll have the comfort of knowing exactly what your payments will be and you'll be able to manage your budget accordingly.

Most mortgages now come with the option to pay your mortgage at a frequency that matches your cash flow — weekly, bi-weekly or semi-monthly. The added benefit of the "accelerated" weekly and bi-weekly payments is that by dividing a regular monthly payment into two or four respectively, and deducting it at the new interval, an extra payment a year is made directly against principal. The surprising effect of this one extra payment a year is to reduce the amortization of the average mortgage by approximately 5 years, with cash savings at the end of your mortgage term.

RENTING A PROPERTY

Rental properties include residential homes, apartment complexes, flats in private homes, condominium units, apartment hotels and furnished suites.

A lease with a fixed term continues as a month-to-month tenancy if the tenant continues to occupy the premises after the lease expired unless both parties have agreed, in writing, that the lease will not automatically be renewed under the RTA.

Damage deposits or security deposits are legal, to cover any damage tenants do to the suite above normal wear and tear, any unpaid rent or bills and any costs if the tenant(s) move out without giving proper notice. If there are no problems, the deposit must be returned with interest. This deposit must be requested when the lease is signed, not later. Nor can it be for more than half of the first months rent. Separate deposits for keys, garage door openers and other items are not allowed.

Vancouver has experienced a surge in the economy recently which has had an impact on the vacancy rates for rental properties.

The average vacancy rate for the Greater Vancouver Regional District rests at aproximately 1.4%. This means that for every 1000 rental units built only 1 unit will be available for rent. This has created a "landlord's" market which causes prices of rentals to escalate. According to the Canadian Mortgage and Housing Commission the average rental price for a 2 bedroom apartment in West Vancouver is close to $1,100.00 per month.

The province of British Columbia currently establishes the maximum amount a landlord may increase rents, through a rent control system.

If these rental controls were to be removed a landlord could charge market value for a property.

The lowest vacancy rates were in the West End and Kerrisdale areas of Vancouver @ 0.4%. The highest vacancy rates were in Surrey at 5.3% and Delta at 6.1%

FINDING AN APARTMENT

Look in every newspaper that serves the Vancouver area. Community newspapers will often have listings not available in the bigger city papers.

When you are looking for an apartment, people may be your best resource. Ask anyone you know who lives in an apartment in the area who their caretaker, landlord or property manager is.

If you are moving to a new area for a job, ask your new employer about the best places to look for an apartment. If you are moving to go to school, talk to the housing office at your school. Most keep lists of local agents and landlords who rent to students.

While there are a number of apartment listing resources on the Web, online resources should definitely not be your only vehicle. Searching these sites, however, will give you an idea what kinds of things are available in your area and what you can expect to pay.

Follow Up Immediately. Especially if you are looking in a tight market, good deals and great apartments are going to go fast.

Be realistic about prices. Look at ads, see what's available, and set your requirements to meet reality. In Vancouver, this may mean paying more than you would like or settling for a smaller place.

INFORMATION

• Apartment Guide
WEB: http://apartmentguide.ca/

• North Shore News (Community Newspaper)
WEB: http://www.nsnews.com/

• The Vancouver Courier (Community Newspaper)
WEB: http://www.vancourier.com/

• 247apartments.com
WEB: http://www.247apartments.com/

• Vancouver online apartments
WEB: http://www.aptrentals.net/

RESPONSIBILITES OF THE LANDLORD

- ensure that all respects of the Tenancy Agreement Regulation be complied to.

- provide the tenant with a written copy of the tenancy agreement no later the 21 days after the agreement has been made.

- sign and date the tenancy agreement

- allow the tenant to inspect the property before signing the tenancy agreement.

- make note of the condition of the property and ensure both the landlord and the tenant have signed copies of this report.

- refund security deposit, plus accrued interest, to tenant, provided premises are left in an acceptable state as agreed to by the landlord and the tenant.

RESPONSIBILITES OF THE TENANT

- sign and date the tenancy agreement

- request landlord provide a written copy of the tenancy agreement within 21 days after the agreement has been made.

- provide the landlord with a security deposit within 30 days of moving into the premises.

- inspect the property prior to signing the tenancy agreement, with the landlord.

- make note of the condition of the property. Have two copies signed by the tenant and the landlord. Tenant keeps one copy, landlord keeps one copy.

- allow all persons residing in the building to continue to enjoy conditions such as reasonable noise levels, cleanliness and respect to personal property.

- return the unit to it's original condition prior to vacating.

- pay rent on time

WHAT TO WATCH FOR

- a tenant can withold rent until a written copy of the tenancy agreement has been provided
- the tenancy agreement must be written in at least 8 point type.
- the agreement must be signed and dated by the tenant and the landlord.
- tenancy agreements can be prepared on any forms as long as the terms of the agreement comply with the ResidentialTenancy Act.
- security deposits are legal.
- a security deposit cannont exceed the value of a half month of the first month's rent.
- a security deposit can only be requested by the landlord at the beginning of a lease.
- a security deposit can be refunded to the tenant at the termination of the tenancy, provided the rental unit was not damaged or the tenant has any outstanding debt with the landlord
- terms such as who is responsible for utiltiy costs, whether parking is included or not, whether pets are allowed or not and specifics on decorating are negotiable between the landlord and the tenant.
- negotiable terms must be agreed upon by both parties.
- a tenant who signs an agreement which would conflict with his/ her rights under the Act can and should, dispute this issue at the Residential tenancy office.
- a tenant under 19 years of age is considered of legal age therefore rules of the act are applicable

CONTACT INFORMATION

- Residential Tenancy Branch
310 - 1190 Melville Street, Vancouver, BC V6E 3W1
Telephone: 604-660-3456
WEB: http://www.pssg.gov.bc.ca/rto/

RENTAL MANAGEMENT COMPANIES

• Bridgestreet Accommodations
Telephone: 1-800-667-8483
WEB: http://www.bridgestreet.com/

• Crosby Property Management Ltd
600 - 777 Hornby Street, Vancouver
Telephone: 604-683-8900
WEB: http://www.crosbypm.com/

• Sunstar Realty Ltd.
6 - 3003 Kingsway, Vancouver
Telephone: 604- 436-1335
WEB: http://www.mybcrental.com/

• The Pacific Sands Apartments
1122 Gilford Street,
Telephone: 604-688-1094
WEB: http://www.pacific-sands.com/

• Vancouver Relocation Services
670 - 999 West Broadway, Vancouver
Telephone: 604-318-2497
WEB: http://www.vancouverrelocation.com/

• YWCA Hotel/Residence
733 Beatty Street
Telephone: 604-895-5830
WEB: http://www.ywcahotel.com

REAL ESTATE

• Dan Campbell, RE/MAX Crest Realty
Telephone: 604-808-8100
WEB: http://www.dancampbell.net/

• Christine Louw, RE/MAX Masters Realty
Telephone: 604-990-3936
WEB: http://www.christinelouw.com/

For more listings of rental management companies and real estate firms consult a yellow pages guide.

• Suzette Costello, Sutton Heritage West Realty, Ltd.
Telephone: 604-267-3800
WEB: http://www.replace.com/can/jchamish/

• Steve Jamieson, RE/MAX Westside
Telephone: 604-961-1648
WEB: http://www.therealestatespot.com/

FURNITURE RENTAL

Get quotes from several furniture rental companies. Pricing often depends on the amount of inventory sitting idle in a warehouse.

Negotiate. If this is not an option ask the salesperson if the inventory list has been prepared using the highest quality items. They may be able to provide you with the same type of item at a lower monthly cost if you go with a lower quality product.

TIPS

Option to buy? If there is a possibility that you may want to purchase the furniture at the end of the term, ask the price of the furniture upfront.

Watch the bait and switch. Make sure the furniture that is delivered is exactly what the salesperson promised. If not, it's well within your rights to demand a replacement, or at the very least, a discount.

Note any dings and dents. The furniture should come to you in good condition. Checking it before the delivery people leave ensures that they have noted the damage as well, if there is any.

The rental company delivers, sets up and removes the furniture when you move.

FURNITURE RENTAL COMPANIES

• Rentown,
587 E Broadway,
Telephone: 604-873-0224

• RTO Centers Rent To Own,
1690 Kingsway,
Telephone: 604-876-9090

• Fibre Wick Creations
419 - 1952 Kingsway Ave. Port Coquitlam
Telephone: 604-878-1803

INSURANCE

Homeowners, condominium owners and renters should be insured.

Tenants can insure their contents by purchasing a "tenant's content package." Tenants are not responsible for insuring the building or structural items in the rental unit.

• Capital Coast Insurance
Telephone: 604-388-8686
WEB: http://www.coastcapitalsavings.com/

• VanCity Credit Union
Offers one stop shopping for all your insurance needs.
Telephone: 604-877-7400
WEB: http://www.vancity.com/

In 1969, Vancouver was granted an expansion NHL Ice Hockey club. The team was named the Canucks after the 1950s superhero, Johnny Canuck.

APARTMENT SEARCHERS NEED TO KNOW LIST

Searching for an apartment can become confusing. If you spend a few days looking at apartments, you may begin to forget the details of some of the ones you have been to.

This list should help keep things clearer.

- Air Conditioning
- Appliances
- Balcony
- Cable TV
- Can your Furniture fit
- Closets & Storage Space
- Damage Deposit
- Dining Room Area
- Does Apartment need Painting
- Elevator or Stairs
- Garbage Disposal & Recycling
- High Speed Internet Access
- Kitchen Space
- Laundry Facilities
- Pets alloved
- Rent Control
- Security on Building
- Type of Heat
- Utilities Included
- Windows

Try to see the units in the daytime. You'll want to know how much natural light an apartment gets. It's helpful to see what shape the place is in and whether more work is needed to make it habitable.

Cover the bases. Many landlords will want to verify your references. Phone ahead to alert possible references, including your former land-lord, that they may receive a call.

BUDGETING YOUR RELOCATION

INCOME

- Commissions
- Investments
- Salary
- Other

HOME RENTAL COSTS

- Deposit
- Insurance
- Rent per month

HOME OWNERSHIP COSTS

- Homeowner's Insurance
- Maintenance
- Mortgage per month
- Property Taxes per year
- Renovations
- Pool, Garden, etc.
- Other

UTILITIES

- Cable
- Electricity
- Garbage
- Gas
- Telephone
- Water
- Other

INSURANCE

- Auto
- Health
- Life
- RRSP
- Other

HOUSEHOLD EXPENSES

- Clothing
- Entertainment
- Food
- Schooling
- Other

TRANSPORTATION

- Auto Loan
- Auto Maintenance
- Gas (Auto)
- Public Transit
- Other

INFORMATION

Statistics Canada
WEB: http://www.statcan.ca/

Cost of Living Reports
WEB: http://relocatecanada.com/crseri.html

Vancouver Economic Development Commission
WEB: http://www.vancouvereconomic.com/

CHAPTER 6: MOVING

MOVING COMPANIES

Get references from friends and other people you trust before choosing a moving company. Moving companies set their own standards.If someone has recommended a company to you ask them why they preferred this company.

Call at least two movers and have them come to your home. Show them in detail what you are moving and give them precise instructions on the services you require (i.e., packing, appliance service, valuation) and have them each provide you with a written, guaranteed estimate. This is important because in many jurisdictions the mover can hold your furniture until their bill is paid in full. Without that written guarantee you have no price certainty. Pick a mover who will provide service and affordability.

Movers generally do not pack anything that is physically attached to the home so if you have items such as paper towel holders, light fixtures and drape tracks that are attached to the home, take them down and leave them nearby. There are also some chemical, corrosive and flammable items that the movers cannot take. In a case where the mover is doing the packing, leave these items where they are. When the packers are finished, go through the home and collect the non admissible items.

Designate an area such as a closet and mark on the door "do not pack".

Place everything that you do not want packed in this closet, for example, keys, important papers or perhaps a child's "special toy".

DO IT YOURSELF

Use sturdy cartons with flaps that completely seal the carton. Mark the cartons with your name, the room the contents came from, and the contents with indelible marker. Pack heavy items (books and tools) in smaller cartons and lighter, bulkier items (bedding, clothes) in larger cartons.

Movers are only responsible for items they pack themselves. If something is broken in a carton you have packed and the carton has no obvious damage (a puncture for example), the mover is not responsible. That is why many people have the mover pack breakable items while they pack the rest.

On moving day ensure the walkways are cleared of snow and debris. When the truck arrives make sure that small children are away from the walkway, door and the moving truck. When carrying items movers have reduced visibility, especially around their feet. The last thing they are looking out for is "little people." This is not their responsibility, they are counting on your help.

The driver is the foreman for the moving company. He will take an inventory of your contents and give everything an identification number. The inventory list will include the condition your furniture is in.

Jade became the official mineral emblem of B.C. in 1968. Consisting mostly of nephrite, B.C. jade is prized by carvers of fine jewellery and sculptures at home and particularly in the Orient. It is mined in many parts of British Columbia.

If you are not sure what condition is being marked against your furniture or you disagree with the driver, ask him to explain or clarify. You will be asked to sign his list.

When loading is complete, ask the driver to accompany you in a tour around the home to make sure no items are being left behind.

The driver will provide you with an inventory check-off sheet so that you have an itemized list of items as they are brought into your home. Ask the driver and his associates to call out the number of items as they are loading them into the house for your own verification.

Let electronic appliances such as PC's and TV's acclimatize to the home before turning them on.

Make note of any new damages or items not checked off on the inventory before the driver leaves. This will strengthen your cargo claim.

Arrangements can be made with the moving company to have assistance unpacking. This is done by either the driver on the day of the move or by a destination agent the following day.

Have a professional company prepare your appliances for shipping. Have the appliance technician certify the condition and working order. This will strengthen your claim if the appliance is not working at your new destination.

If you have a cargo claim contact the destination agent as soon as possible.

INFORMATION

• Royal Moving & Storage
Telephone: 1-800-361-1634
WEB: http://www.royalmoving.com/

• Outaouais Moving Inc.
Telephone: 1-800-361-1634
WEB: http://www.outaouaismoving.com/

• Two Small Men with Big Hearts Moving Company
Telephone: 1-800-727-6255

• Super Movers Local & Long Distance
Telephone: 604-808-2588

• St. George Moving & Storage
Telephone: 604-520-1900

MOVING PLANNER

FOUR TO SIX WEEKS BEFORE YOUR MOVE

• Clean out your closets, attic, basement, cupboards, toy chests and bookshelves. Discard anything you don't want or need.

• Consider having a tag or garage sale.

• Donate unwanted items to charitable organizations.

• Arrange to collect any advance deposits or security deposits on utilities or rentals.

• Evaluate whether to ship your appliances. Age, size and colour are all considerations.

• Make a complete inventory of items to be moved.

• Decide if you will move all your plants or just your favourites.

• Use up your frozen foods. They CANNOT be safely shipped. It is also advisable to reduce your supply of canned goods.

• Notify the security company, lawn or snow-removal services or any other regular services of your vacating date.

• Notify your post office, publications, and correspondance of your change of address and date of move.

• Check your homeowner's insurance. Be sure to contact a new insurance company in your new province/city.

- Check on club membership fees. The money may be refunded or, if allowed, you might consider transferring/selling the membership to a friend.

- Check with your veterinarian regarding any travel preparation needed for your pets.

- Register children for school; transfer all necessary school records.

- Plan shipment date to occur after closing on your new home.

AT LEAST TWO WEEKS BEFORE THE MOVE

- Contact telephone, electric, gas and water companies to confirm date to discontinue service. Verify this date with your realtor/landlord.

- Advise utility companies in your new location of a start-up date.

- Advise dairy, laundry, newspaper carrier and sanitation service to discontinue services.

- Be sure to clean out school or gymnasium lockers.

- Ask your physician(s) and dentist for referrals. Transfer medical records and get copies of prescriptions.

- Arrange for the transfer of valuables. Check contents of your safe-deposit box. **DO NOT SHIP** any valuables (such as jewelry, insurance policies, legal documents, currency, stamp and coin collections) with the moving company. Either carry them with you or send by insured or certified mail.

- **DO NOT SHIP** combustible or flammable items. These include oil-base paints, bleach, cleaning and lighting fluids, matches and ammunition. All aerosol cans (including hair sprays, shaving creams, deodorants and household cleaners) must be stored away.

ONE WEEK BEFORE THE MOVE

- Keep a detailed record and receipts of your moving expenses for income-tax purposes. This includes transportation, lodging, meals, etc.

- Drain gas and oil from lawn mowers, chain saws, snow blowers, etc. Gas grills and kerosene heaters must be empty. Cars and motorcycles should have only 1/4 tank of gas if they are being shipped.

- Prepare a "ready box" for last on and first off articles in the moving truck. This might include essentials from your kitchen and bathroom. You may also wish to include items such as a hammer, pliers, screwdrivers and nails.

- Prepare a "ready box" with necessary medications and first-aid supplies.

- Prepare a "ready box" for your children with their own special treasures. Include toys, games and snacks.

- Defrost and clean your refrigerator and freezer at least 24 hours in advance of the move.

- Keep your telephone connected during your moving day.

DAY BEFORE THE MOVE

The packing crew usually arrives the day before the van is loaded. Be sure someone is on site to supervise the packing.

• Pack all valuables you want to take with you.

• Fragile items require special attention.

• Gather keys to the house and arrange to leave them with the new owners, your real estate agent, landlord or a trusted neighbor.

 • Notify police if your home will be unoccupied after you leave.

 • Notify a close friend or relative of your itinerary in case of emergency.

DAY OF MOVE OUT

• Check the mover's inventory to be sure you agree with the mover's judgment on the condition of your household goods. Take photographs if there is a dispute.

• Get a copy of the inventory list.

• Load items you are taking with you on the trip, including luggage.

• Search every room before the van leaves.

 • Check the Bill of Lading for completion and accuracy before you sign it. Retain a copy for your records.

• Turn off the water heater. Set the thermostat at 15 degrees celsius.

• Contact utility companies to verify start up dates.

MOVING KIDS AND TEENS

By considering a move in three stages - before, during, and after - and thinking about your children's needs during each stage, you can make a big difference in how your kids feel about the move and how they adjust afterwards.

Tell your children about the move as soon as you can. The more time they have to think about and prepare for the move, the easier it will be for them.

Give your children a chance to express their feelings. Be honest about your own feelings too. Most children experience anger, sadness or worry just as adults do.

Help older children prepare a list of phone numbers and addresses of close friends, relatives, and other important people in their lives. Knowing they can stay in touch with these people is an important part of a successful move.

Let them participate in decision making.

• Packing up and hauling a houseful of furniture to another city or Province is a tough job, but it's nothing compared to moving kids who don't want to leave their home.

"Most parents are pretty insensitive," says a psychologist. "They don't understand the child's point of view. They're so involved in the economics of the move — getting the job, the house. It's hard for them to think of the child's needs." Don't just spring it on them Some parents do a good job of preparing children for relocation, but others just spring it on them — "We're moving!"

"Talk to them in advance. Even at age 3, they may not get the whole concept, but explain how you're moving to a new city and they'll be making new friends." Stick to familiar routines, the same rules hold for older children. Keep as many things constant as possible — and don't forgo discipline. Discipline should be another constant — parents shouldn't bend rules just because they're feeling guilty about causing havoc in the child's life.

VANCOUVER FOR KIDS AND TEENS

Hi there! This is to let you know that Vancouver isn't just for old folks, there are plenty of activities for children and teenagers. We haven't listed everything available, but the following pages gives you an idea about how cool Vancouver really is.

•BC BOYS CHOIR
For boys only... what a pity.
WEB: http://www.bcboyschoir.org/

•BEACHES AND PARKS
Any of Vancouvers beaches and parks are great outdoor spots.
WEB: http://www.city.vancouver.bc.ca/parks/

•CAPILANO SUSPENSION BRIDGE
Now this is really something to tell your friends about.
WEB: http://www.capbridge.com/

•CIRKIDS
Do not run away with the Circus learn it here.
WEB: http://www.cirkids.org/

•CRITTER CARE WILDLIFE SOCIETY
WEB: http://www.bc-alter.net/critter/

•GRANVILLE ISLAND
Cool Place. Always something going on.
WEB: http://www.granville-island.net/

•GROUSE MOUNTAIN RESORT
Your Snowboard Parking lot
WEB: http://www.grousemtn.com/

•HOLLYBURN JACKRABBIT SKI CLUB
WEB: http://www3.telus.net/jackrabbits/

•KART RACING AROUND VANCOUVER
Your own Indy 500
WEB: http://home.portal.ca/~beast/kart.htm

•SCIENCE WORLD
Home to the Alcan OMNIMAX and the Science Theatre.
WEB: http://www.scienceworld.bc.ca/

•MILLENIUM KIDS LEARNING CENTRE
Need some help with Math or English ?
WEB: http://www.millenniumkidscentres.com/

•PACIFIC NATIONAL EXHIBITION
The Cool place to be in the summertime
WEB: http://www.pne.bc.ca/

•PACIFIC SPACE CENTRE
For all aspiring Space Cadets
WEB: http://pacific-space-centre.bc.ca/

•PLAYLAND
Get the ride of your life.
WEB: http://www.pne.bc.ca/

•SKATEBOARDING PARKS
WEB:
http://www.city.vancouver.bc.ca/parks/recreation/skate.htm

•STANLEY PARK
Over 8 million people visit every year.
WEB: http://www.city.vancouver.bc.ca/parks/3.htm

•SWIMMING
Many small pools make a big one.
WEB: http://www.city.vancouver.bc.ca/parks/aquatics.htm

•VANCOUVER AQUARIUM MARINE SCIENCE CENTRE
Coolest Sleepover on the Planet!
WEB: http://www.vanaqua.org/

•VANCOUVER MARITIME MUSEUM
Sail the Tug Boat
WEB: http://www.vmm.bc.ca/

•VANCOUVER TROLLEY COMPANY
Take a trolley, see it all.
WEB: http://www.vancouvertrolley.com/

MOVING WITH PETS

If you are travelling by air contact the airline well in advance to check regulations and services. If you travelling by car make sure your pet does not become motion sick.

Don't feed your pet for several hours prior to your trip. However, have fresh, cool water available and stop frequently for drinks and walks.

Keep birds and small pets - such as hamsters – in their cages. Make sure the cages are well ventilated yet protected from drafts.

If you are bringing pets into Canada, there are some guidelines you must follow. Cats and dogs entering Canada from the United States must have a Health Certificate issued seven days prior to entry into Canada as well as all routine immunizations. An original certificate of rabies vaccinations should accompany the health certificate. Customs also requires a freedom of rabies form to accompany the pet.

This certificate should be issued by the pet's veterinarian and should show proof that the rabies shot was administered more than 30 days prior but not more than 180 days prior to your departure.

Countries that are considered to be rabies free require only that a certificate of origin and a freedom from rabies form be filled out. These countries are considered rabies free: Sweden, Norway, Northen Ireland, Ireland and Great Britain. Pets should have identification tags and rabies tags.

No quarantine or import permits are required if the proper papers accompany the pet. Seeing eye dogs may enter without restriction.

If a dog is less than three months old, but older than eight weeks old, and the puppy is traveling with you, a certificate of vaccination and a rabies vaccination must be provided.

If a dog is less than three months old, but older than eight weeks old, and is traveling unaccompanied, proof of vaccination must be provided for the following: hepatitis, parvovirue, parainfluenza and distemper. If a dog is older than three months, a rabies vaccination and certificate of vaccination must be provided. Any vaccinations that have been administered in the past three years prior to moving will be accepted with proof.

The age of the pet must be noted on the required paperwork. Animals may enter the country without the proper paperwork as long as the Ministry receives the information within a two-week period of arrival. The general rule for bringing pets into the country is set at a limit of two dogs per person. If a person is emigrating, the limit can be raised to allow up to five animals but this must be approved.

You may import up to two pet birds if they are accompanied by their owner and are certified to have been in the owners possession and isolated from other birds for the preceding 90 days.

Horses and other domestic animals may be brought into Canada but it is best to speak to the Chief of Imports, Animal Health Division for information regarding this issue.

The fees for inspection of the paperwork by Customs is $ 30.00 (thirty) for the first pet and $5.00 (five) for the second pet (if applicable). If the animal has entered the country without papers the fee doubles. All certificates must be in either English or French - no other languages will be accepted.

• Animal Health Division
Telephone: 604-666-8750
WEB: http://www.inspection.gc.ca/

DEDUCTIBLE MOVING EXPENSES

Some moving expenses may be tax deductible.

- moving within Canada to a new location to start a job
- moving within Canada to start a business
- moving within Canada to attend full-time courses at a post-secondary institution.
- if your new home is at least 40 km closer to your to your new place of work
- if your new home is at least 40 km closer to your to your new school

DEDUCTIONS

- vehicle expenses, meals and accommodation during travel time
- cost of cancelling a lease at your previous residence
- transportation and storage of personal effects
- 15 days maximum for meals and accommodation near either residence if your moving dates do not coincide.
- selling costs of your residence including real estate commission, mortgage penalty and advertising.
- legal fees on the sale and purchase of your properties.
- legal fees and land transfer tax for new property.
- utilitiy disconnection/reconnection costs.

 These deductions are limited to income earned at the new location. Your deduction is reduced by any reimbursement received from your employer.

 It is best to consult with a professional who knows eligibility rules and any new changes in policy.

 You can find the newest form and rules here:

WEB:

http://www.ccra-adrc.gc.ca/E/pbg/tf/t1-meq/README.html

http://www.ccra-adrc.gc.ca/formspubs/menu-e.html

CHAPTER 7: TRANSPORTATION

DRIVING IN BRITISH COLUMBIA

If you are new to B.C. and drive a vehicle, you need to obtain a B.C. driver's license within 90 days after moving here.

To obtain a BC driver's license, you need to provide proof of the length of time you have previously held a driver's license.

PROOF OF DRIVING EXPERIENCE

In most cases, your out-of-province driver's license is sufficient to show proof of your driving experience. ICBC uses the "Issue Date" shown on the license to calculate the length of time you have been eligible to drive. If you've held a license for 18 months and your out-of-province license was recently renewed, the "Issue Date" shown may not be sufficient to indicate you've held a license for 18 months. In this case, you will need to contact your previous jurisdiction and obtain proof of the length of time you have been licensed.

Canadian, American, Austrian, German, Japanese or Korean driver's license?

You will be issued a new equivalent class B.C. driver's license. In most cases, you will not need to take a road test if you hold:

• a Canadian or American passenger car or motorcycle operator's license,

• an Austrian or German Category B or German Class 3 driver's license for passenger cars,

• a Japanese Ordinary driver's licence or a Korean Class 2 Ordinary driver's licence for passenger cars,

• a Canadian license equivalent to a B.C. Class 1, 2, 3 or 4 (commercial) license and your license is valid or expired less than 3 years ago.

DRIVER & VEHICLE SERVICES/ROAD TESTS

HERE'S THE PROCESS:

1. Review the appropriate ICBC driving guide, listed below:

- RoadSense for Drivers (for Class 5, 7 or 7L — passenger vehicles)

- Tuning Up (for Class 5 or 7 — passenger vehicles)

- RoadSense for Riders (for Class 6, 8 or 8L — motorcycles)

- Tuning Up for Riders (for Class 6 or 8 — motorcycles)

- Driving Commercial Vehicles (for Class 1, 2, 3 or 4).

Review the ICBC driving guide which is available at any ICBC driver licensing office. Driver training programs are available through many different companies.

2. Take your current license and two pieces of identification (one with picture id) i.e. passport, to any driver licensing office.

3. The knowledge test and vision screening can be done at any time

4. Make an appointment for your road test

To check current fees for these services:

Telephone: 1-800-663-3051
WEB: http://www.icbc.com

DRIVER'S LICENSE

1. Take your license and one piece of primary and secondar identifi cation to any driver licensing office. You may also be required to provide a translation of your driver's license.

Primary identification would include:

- Birth certificate
- B.C. Identification card (new digital style only)
- Canadian Citizenship Identification
- Canada Identity Card issued by Foreign Affairs Canada

Secondary identification would include:

- Passport
- Canadian or other Driver's license
- Naturalization certificate
- Canadian Forces identification
- Police identification
- Foreign Affairs Canada or consular identification

2. Answer some traffic safety awareness questions (you may wish to review "Road Sense for Drivers" available at an ICBC driver licensing office).

3. Undergo a vision screening and answer questions relative to your medical and physical fitness. You may also be asked to fill out a medical form.

4. Your photo is taken. Smile! You now have a new B.C. driver's license. There is a fee for this service.

INFORMATION

- Driver Services Centre
4126 MacDonald Street Vancouver, B.C., V6L 2P2
Telephone: 604-661-2255

GRADUATED LICENSING IN BC (NEW DRIVERS)

B.C.'s driver licensing process is intended to produce safe, careful drivers. The standards are among the strictest in North America. Driving is complex. Gaining the necessary skills and experience takes time.

Special restrictions are placed on the new learner to ensure enough road experience and confidence is gained at a minimal risk to both the driver and other drivers on the road.

It's like an apprenticeship. You get the on-road experience you need, but with special restrictions on your license that help to reduce your risks. As you gain skills and experience, these restrictions are removed. For new drivers, getting your full privilege Class 5 drivers license generally takes about two years. You are eligible to apply for your drivers license when you turn 16.

The government of British Columbia has a website that will provide you with information about driving in B.C.

• Graduated Licensing Program
Telephone: 1-800-950-1498
WEB: http://www.icbc.com/

VEHICLE REGISTRATION AND INSPECTION

Register, license and insure any vehicle you bring to B.C. within 30 days of its arrival here. (Vehicles intended for commercial use must be registered, licensed and insured immediately.)

You have up to 90 days to get your B.C. driver's license.

Most used vehicles (other than trailers or motorcycles) registered in B.C. for the first time or returning to B.C. after being registered outside the province must pass a mechanical safety inspection at a designated B.C. inspection facility before they can be registered, licensed and insured.

Rebuilt, altered or constructed vehicles (including kit vehicles) require a structural inspection along with the mechanical safety inspection.

A list of inspection facilities is available from Autoplan brokers or driver licensing offices. When your vehicle has passed the inspection take your vehicle and a copy of the inspection report as well as your current registration to an Autoplan broker. The broker must be able to visually check the Vehicle Identification Number (VIN.)

The western red cedar was adopted as the official tree of the province on February 18, 1988. Historically, the tree has played a key role in the lives of west coast aboriginal people, and continues to be a valuable resource for the province.

INSURANCE

 A broker will assist you with insurance arrangements. B.C. has a mandatory insurance plan, ICBC, which all drivers must have. ICBC, a crown corporation, works with the provincial government to ensure all drivers are insured. ICBC provides a driver with the minimum amount of insurance required. Autoplan, the insurance broker for ICBC, can also arrange extra insurance or you can purchase extra insurance from a private broker.

INFORMATION

• ICBC, Insurance Corporation of British Columbia
Telephone: 1-800-663-3051 **From Canada and USA**
WEB: http://www.icbc.com/

• John Ross Insurance Service Ltd.
1829 West Broadway, Vancouver, V6J 1Y5
Telephone: 604-731-5258
WEB: http://www.johnrossinsurance.com/

• BC Automobile Association
Telephone: 604-268-5600
WEB: http://www.bcaa.com/

• Air Care Program
Telephone: 604-433-5633
WEB: http://www.aircare.ca/

You must have a B.C. driver's license for identification when you are ready to purchase your insurance if you plan to take advantage of Autoplan 12. Autoplan 12 is ICBC's financing program which lets you pay for the annual insurance policy in 12 monthly payments. If you don't have a B.C. driver's license or any recent history with ICBC, you will have to start out on Autoplan 6 if you want financing for your premium.

IMPORTED VEHICLES

Importing a vehicle into British Columbia is governed by the federal government. Transport Canada sets the guidelines for all vehicles entering Canada from the U.S. and other parts of the world. The list of admissible vehicles is quite extensive.

The following is a very brief overview of vehicles permitted to be imported into Canada, at this time.

• 1986 to 1990 Chryslers permitted include the:
• Plymouth, Dodge and Eagle 1986 400/600 2 door
• 1989 Acclaim,
• 1990 Colt and
• 1987 Sundance.

• 1991 to 2002 Chryslers not permitted include the:
• 1994 and 1995 LeBaron sedan
• 1991 and 1992 Monaco
• 1992 to 1996 Viper Roadster

Transport Canada has the full listing of vehicles that are and are not admissible at their web site which we have included here.

• Registrar of Imported Vehicles
Telephone: 1-888-848-8240
WEB: http://www.riv.ca/

• Canada Customs & Revenue Agency
Telephone: 204-983-3500
WEB: http://www.ccra-adrc.gc.ca/

• Transport Canada
Telephone: 613-990-2309
WEB: http://www.tc.gc.ca/

PUBLIC TRANSIT

The Greater Vancouver Transportation Authority, also known as "TransLink", was created by the BC Greater Vancouver Transportation Authority Act in 1998.

TransLink's subsidiary companies and contractors provide the following services: Public transit - buses, SeaBus, SkyTrain, West Coast Express and HandyDART Albion Ferry AirCare, and promoting transportation alternatives such as cycling and carpooling.

TRANSLINK FARES

Fares vary depending on the time of day, day of the week and the distance you travel. Fares may be paid by cash or by purchasing tickets or passes before you travel. When boarding Translink, cash fares must be paid in exact change.

Regular fares are in effect weekdays from the start of the service day to 6:30 pm. During regular hours, the service area is divided into three zones. The fare you pay depends on the number of zones in which you travel.

Discounted fares are in effect weekdays after 6:30 pm to the end of the service day, all day Saturday, Sunday and holidays. During discount hours, zone boundaries do not apply.

Children 5 to 13 years, secondary students 14 to 19 years with valid GoCard, seniors 65+ with proof of age and HandyPass holders are eligible to travel at "Concession" fares.

Children 4 years and younger ride for free. Adult fares on Translink are the same as for buses including the West Vancouver Blue buses, SkyTrain and SeaBus.

• For Current Fare Information
Telephone: 604-953-3333
WEB: http://www.translink.bc.ca/

TRANSIT TICKETS

Faresaver Tickets can be purchased for One, Two or Three Zones and can be purchased in advance in booklets of 10. They must be validated at a ticket machine before boarding SkyTrain and SeaBus. One Zone Concession tickets are also available in books of 10.

A day pass is good for one day's unlimited travel. DayPasses with "scratch-off" date selection may be purchased in advance at FareDealer outlets. There is a DayPass ticket machine at the Tsawwassen Ferry Terminal. DayPasses are sold at ticket machines at the SeaBus and SkyTrain stations on the day of travel.

A monthly pass is available in One, Two or Three Zone and Concession fares. FareCards are valid for unlimited travel during the month shown and are transferable.

Tickets and monthly FareCard passes are sold at 7-Elevens, Safeways and Scotia Banks (Scotia Banks sell monthly passes only). Look for the Fare Dealer symbol at London Drugs, Mac's and other convenience stores. FareCards are sold the last 5 and the first 5 working days of each month. FareSaver tickets and Day Passes are available throughout the month.

FareCards are also available after the 5th of the month at the FareDealer outlet at Gateway Station, 108 Avenue at 134th Street in Surrey, (mezzanine floor) between 8 AM and 4 PM weekdays (excluding holidays).

GOCARDS FOR HIGH SCHOOL STUDENTS

The GoCard is for secondary school students, aged 14 to 19, in grades 8 though 12. A GoCard entitles the registered user to "Concession" fares, and must be presented whenever boarding a transit vehicle.

Applications for the GoCard are available through high school offices.

FAST TRAX DISCOUNT FARES

FastTrax is a discount system for full-time students attending approved post-secondary institutions. With a Fast Trax Transit Strip attached to a valid student I.D., post secondary students can travel throughout the system anytime on a regularly-priced adult one-zone monthly FareCard. FastTrax Stickers are available at most student union associations. A small fee may be applied. Both student I.D. and one-zone monthly FareCard must be shown when boarding and when requested.

TRANSFERS

If you pay cash on a bus, and wish to change to another bus, SkyTrain or SeaBus, ask your operator for a transfer when you board. Transfers are valid for 90 minutes of travel in any direction. Fare receipts and validated FareSaver tickets also serve as transfers. Cash-fare passengers travelling more than one zone should always request a transfer and keep it as proof of payment. When you are issued a fare receipt or transfer, it will be colour coded to show the number of zones you have purchased.

PROOF OF PAYMENT

Proof of payment is a valid transfer, fare receipt, validated FareSaver ticket or pass. You must carry proof of payment when transferring from one transit vehicle to another, when crossing zone boundaries and at all times while in a Fare Paid Zone. An operator or attendant may ask to see your proof of payment at any time.

MODES OF TRANSPORTATION

SKYTRAIN

SkyTrain's Expo Line trains operate from Waterfront to King George Station. The line runs along a scenic 28 kilometer track from Vancouver to Burnaby, New Westminster, and Surrey in just 39 minutes. There are currently 20 stations along this route. Four downtown stations are underground and marked at street level. The other 16 are elevated and visible from the street.

Millennium Line trains make the same stops from Waterfront to Columbia, before branching to Sapperton, Braid, Lougheed Town Centre and beyond to Commercial Drive, adjacent to the existing Broadway Station.

SkyTrain links with a network of buses at many stations and with SeaBus at Waterfront Station in downtown Vancouver. Daily service is provided every three to five minutes.

WEB: http://www.rapidtransit.bc.ca/

WEST COAST EXPRESS

West Coast Express is a premium commuter rail service linking Mission, Port Haney, Maple Ridge, Pitt Meadows, Port Coquitlam, Coquitlam and Port Moody with downtown Vancouver.

They operate Monday to Friday during peak periods to get you to your destination, quickly, comfortably and inexpensively.

WEB: http://www.westcoastexpress.com/

HANDYDART

HandyDART is TransLink's shared-ride, custom transit system, operated by private agencies throughout the Lower Mainland. Lift-equipped vans provide door-to-door transportation for passengers in wheelchairs and others with disabilities that restrict mobility.

ALBION FERRY

As a subsidiary of TransLink, Fraser River Marine Transportation is responsible for providing ferry service for vehicles and walk-on passengers across the Fraser River between Maple Ridge and Fort Langley.

The ferries operate daily between 5:15 am and 1:15 am, at approximately fifteen minute intervals during the day and half hour intervals during the late evenings. It takes only 10 minutes to get across the river.

• Translink Transit information
Telephone: 604-953-3333
WEB: http://www.translink.bc.ca/

AIRLINES

• Air Canada
Telephone: 1-800-667-1729
WEB: http://www.aircanada.ca/

• Air Canada Jazz
Telephone: 1-800-538-5696
WEB: http://www.aircanadajazz.com/

• Foreign Airlines
WEB: http://relocatecanada.com/airlines.html

• Harbour Air
Telephone: 1-800-665-0212
WEB: http://www.harbour-air.com/

• Helijet Airways
Telephone: 250-382-6222
WEB: http://www.helijet.com/

• Kenmore Air
Telephone: 1-800-543-9595
WEB: http://www.kenmoreair.com/

• Pacific Coastal Airlines
Telephone: 1-800-663-2872
WEB: http://www.pacific-coastal.com/

• West Coast Air
Telephone: 1-800-347-2222
WEB: http://www.westcoastair.com/

• WestJet
Telephone: 1-800-538-5696
WEB: http://westjet.com/

BUS

• Coast Mountain Bus Company
Telephone: 604-540-3000
WEB: http://www.coastmountainbus.com/

• Greyhound Canada
Telephone: 1-800-661-8747
WEB: http://www.greyhound.ca/

• Pacific Coach Lines
Telephone: 604-662-7575
WEB: http://www.pacificcoach.com/

FERRIES

• BC Ferries
Telephone: 250-386-3431
WEB: http://www.bcferries.bc.ca/

• Vancouver Port Authority
Telephone: 604-665-9000
WEB: http://www.portvancouver.com/

RAIL

• Amtrak
WEB: http://www.amtrak.com/

• BC Rail
Telephone: 604-984-5246
WEB: http://www.bcrail.com/

• Via Rail
Telephone: 1-800-561-8630
WEB: http://www.viarail.ca/

• West Coast Express
Telephone: 604-488-8906
WEB: http://www.westcoastexpress.com/

CHAPTER 8: EMPLOYMENT

IMMIGRATION

Canada is renowned for it's "open door policy" with regard to immigration. The September 11, 2001 attack on the World Trade Centre in New York dramatically changed the immigration procedure in Canada. Some of these changes have already been established such as the requirement of a permanent resident card, for all immigrants arriving in Canada.

If this is a corporate move, your company should be knowledgeable about Immigration Canada's policies for transferees.

The immigration department will want to know the following information relating to your new job. This must be done prior to accepting an offer to relocate.

- a letter from your employer indicating your new position
- how long you have been working in this position (this must be a miniumum of one year in most cases)
- a clear and concise job description
- specialized knowledge you possesses that enable you to fill this position
- relationship between the two companies that you are transferring to and from.

Most corporate transferees are permitted to remain in the country for a maximum of three years. Employment Authorizations are issued to transferees on a temporary bases.

Your employer in Canada must provide details of the prospective job position to the Human Resources Development Canada Centre to request a job validation. Once this has been approved the Human Resources Development Canada Centre may authorize the job offer.

EMPLOYMENT AUTHORIZATION

An employment authorization is issued for a specific job after the job offer has been approved by Human Resources Development Canada (HRDC).

If you are applying for your employment authorization outside Canada, you must submit the application to a visa office at a Canadian embassy, high comission or consulate abroad.

Prior to submitting your application, contact the visa office to see if you are required to fill out any additional forms or provide any additional documents. You will need the following:

- a completed application form IMM1295
- a confirmation of offer of employment form 5056 that has been prepared by your employer and validated by a Canada Employment Centre
- a written job offer or contract from your prospective employer in Canada which describes your intended position
- the length of time that you have been doing this job in your current place of employment.

The fees for applying for citizenship and immigration do change.

For the most recent updates go to this website.

WEB: http://www.cic.gc.ca/english/applications/fees.html
Telephone: Outside Canada: + 604-666-2171
Telephone: Vancouver Area: 604-666-2171
Telephone: Across Canada: 1-888-242-2100

STUDENT VISA

If you are a student wanting to study in Canada you must have authorization to receive academic, vocational or professional training in Canada. Students may be issued authorization which is valid for the duration of their program.

The student must have already enrolled in a government-approved academic institution, paid their tuition fees and received acceptance into their program by the academic institution and have working knowledge of English or French in order to be able to follow the course curriculum. These criteria must be met prior to submitting an application for a Student Authorization to a Canadian visa post abroad.

WORK VISA

If you are entering Canada and you are a citizen of either the United States or the United Kingdom, you are not required to have a visa. If you are certain that your stay in Canada will be longer than six months but not as long as thirty-six months, you must register and declare your intention to the examining officer upon your entry into Canada.

If your term of employment is expected to last longer than thirty-six months, contact the Immigration department prior to your departure for Canada.

SOCIAL INSURANCE NUMBER (SIN)

Besides having immigration documents, you will be required to have the following documents during your stay. Some you will need immediately, your social insurance number for example, while others can wait for a month or two. These documents include proof of citizenship, a passport and, as mentioned earlier, your social insurance number.

You must have a SIN to be put on a company payroll.

Application for your SIN can be done at the Human Resources Development Centre of Canada offices. It is possible to apply through the mail, however, original documents are required and HRDC is not responsible for any lost paperwork. This can be very frustrating because these documents will have to be replaced.

• Vancouver Human Resource Centre Canada
125 Est 10th Avenue, Vancouver, BC, V5T 1Z3
Telephone: 604-872-7431
WEB: http://www.hrdc-drhc.gc.ca/sin/

LOOKING FOR EMPLOYMENT

RESOURCES FOR PROSPECTIVE JOB HUNTERS

The internet is an excellent resource to explore job options. Local newspapers and national newspapers include help wanted ads. The Human Resources Development Canada Centre has several offices in the Greater Vancouver Area.

WEB:
http://workinfonet.bc.ca/
http://www.allvanjobs.com/
http://www.monster.ca
http://www.bcjobs.net/
http://relocatecanada.com/jobs.html

• Burnaby Human Resource Centre Canada
4980 Kingsway - Suite 300, Burnaby, B.C., V5H 4G1
Telephone: 604-437-3761
WEB: http://www.bc.hrdc-drhc.gc.ca/5615/index_e.shtml

• Coquitlam Human Resource Centre Canada
2963 Glen Drive, Suite 100, Coquitlam, B.C., V3B 2P7
Telephone: 604-464-7144
WEB: http://www.bc.hrdc-drhc.gc.ca/5615/index_e.shtml

• North Shore Human Resource Centre Canada
1111 Lonsdale Avenue., 2nd Flr. North Vancouver, B.C., V7M 2H4
Telephone: 604-988-1151
WEB: http://www.bc.hrdc-drhc.gc.ca/5614/index_e.shtml

• Richmond Human Resource Centre Canada
301-4940 Number 3 Road, Richmond, B.C., V6X 3A5
Telephone: 604-273-6431
WEB: http://www.bc.hrdc-drhc.gc.ca/5615/index_e.shtml

• Human Resource Centre Canada, main web Site for BC/Yukon
WEB: http://www.bc.hrdc-drhc.gc.ca/

• Sinclair Centre HRCC
415 - 757 West Hastings Street
Telephone: 604-681-8253
WEB:http://www.bc.hrdc-drhc.gc.ca/5615/index_e.shtml

• Surrey Human Resource Centre Canada
7404 King George Hwy., Surrey, B.C., V3W 0L4
Telephone: 604-590-3346
WEB: http://www.bc.hrdc-drhc.gc.ca/5616/index_e.shtml

• Vancouver Human Resource Centre Canada
125 East 10th Avenue, Vancouver, B.C., V5T 1Z3
Telephone: 604-872-7431
WEB: http://www.bc.hrdc-drhc.gc.ca/5615/index_e.shtml

• Vancouver Human Resource Centre Canada Hastings
757 Hastings Street West, Suite 415, Vancouver, B.C., V6C 1A1
Telephone: 604-681-8253
WEB: http://www.bc.hrdc-drhc.gc.ca/5615/index_e.shtml

• Vancouver Human Resource Centre Canada, Tenth Avenue
125 East 10th Avenue, Vancouver
Telephone: 604-872-7431
WEB: http://www.bc.hrdc-drhc.gc.ca/5615/index_e.shtml

Human Resources Development Canada is to help Canadians participate fully in the workplace and the community. Delivering a wide range of programs and services in more than 320 offices across the country.

BORDER CROSSING

Citizens of the United States crossing the Canadian border must provide proof of citizenship. You will be required to show a U.S. passport, an original U.S. birth certificate or U.S. naturalization papers. These three documents are the only acceptable forms of identification. A permanent resident from the United States but not a U.S. citizen must have an Alien Registration Card.

Travellers to Canada from areas outside of the U.S. must have a valid national passport. Parents who are divorced or separated must have proof of legal custody, such as custody papers and a birth certificate, if their child is travelling with them. This applies to any child under the age of 18. Questions can be directed to the Canadian Embassy, High Commission or Consulate responsible for your region.

It is certain there will continue to be changes to immigration policies. We suggest you visit the following web site to obtain the latest information.

WEB: http://www.cic.gc.ca/

Telephone: From USA: 1-800-992-7037
Telephone: In Canada: 1-888-242-2100
Telephone: In Vancouver: 604-666-2171

B.C.'s total land and freshwater area is 95 million hectares,larger than France and Germany combined. Only 30 countries are larger. British Columbia occupies about 10 per cent of Canada's land surface.

STATUTORY HOLIDAYS

A legal holiday (a day off with pay) for qualified employees.

• New Year's Day	January 1
• Good Friday	April 18 (2003)
• Easter Monday	April 21 (2003)
• Victoria Day	Monday preceding May 25
• Canada Day	July 1
• British Columbia Day	First Monday in August
• Labour Day	First Monday of September
• Thanksgiving Day	Second Monday of October
• Remembrance Day	November 11
• Christmas Day	December 25

• Easter Sunday, Easter Monday and Boxing Day are not statutory holidays

ELIGIBILITY

• you must have been employed for at least 30 calendar days.

INFORMATION

• B.C. Statutory Holidays to 2005
WEB: http://www.labour.gov.bc.ca/esb/facshts/stats.htm

DID YOU KNOW

That the Kwakiutl of central British Columbia were and still are some of the most innovative totem carvers. Their poles are elaborate and brightly painted.

TAXES

Canadian residents are required to pay tax on any income world-wide. Retirement pension funds are not taxed. If you are considered a non-resident you are still required to pay tax on your Canadian income. A non-resident is defined as someone who

- owns a Canadian residence
- has a spouse and/or dependants
- has personal property
- has economic interests and social ties.

You are a resident if you have spent 183 days or more in a calendar year in Canada, regardless of where the permanent residence is.

Federal income tax ranges from 16% of total income to a maximum of 53.19%. Income tax is also payable on a provincial level. In British Columbia the tax rates range from a minimum of 7.3% to a maximum of 16.7%.

The federal government receives all tax revenue and disperses it to each province. Quebec handles its own collection and disbursement.

Canada Customs and Revenue Agency does allow tax deductions on personal and business income tax. Business expenses can be used to reduce taxable income and include such items as travel, union or professional dues, and home office equipment. It is wise to ensure that the deductions can be made prior to filing your tax return. The criteria change frequently so we have included a website for your further reference.

- Canada Customs and Revenue Agency
WEB: http://www.ccra-adrc.gc.ca

- British Columbia Ministry of Finance
WEB: http://www.gov.bc.ca/fin/

GST: GOODS AND SERVICES TAX

The goods and services tax, also known as GST, is a federal tax. It is applied in all cases when a service has been provided to the purchaser.For example, if you go to a hair salon to get a hair cut, you have been provided a service. Therefore the salon must charge you GST on the total bill. At the time of publishing this book the GST rate is 7.0%

PST: PROVINCIAL SALES TAX

The provincial sales tax, also known as PST, is, as the name implies, a provincially based tax.

In British Columbia the rate for the PST is 7.5%. Taxes are paid on most items that one would purchase except for basic groceries and children's clothing.

Grocery items such as pet food and other "luxury items" or non - essential items are taxable.

In British Columbia, the combined tax rate is 14.5%, with the PST at 7.5% and the GST at 7%. This can add up to quite a difference to the original price.

This is unlike Great Britain which includes the VAT (value added tax) in the price of an item on the shelf.

INFORMATION PST:

· The taxpayer information line,
Telephone: 604-660-4524
WEB: http://www.rev.gov.bc.ca/ctb/taxablesrvcs.htm

CHAPTER 9, CULTURAL CONNECTIONS

VANCOUVER CULTURE

The traditional history of Canada is of French and British heritage. Obviously, prior to arrival of the French and British explorers in Canada,the country was populated by several different native Indian tribes.

The two cultures of French and British heritage lived in relative harmony during most of the 1800-1900s. The western prairies of Canada were becoming more populated in the late 1800s as the federal government was offering free land to anyone who would settle there. Progress and growth led to the need for faster and more efficient transportation than the horse and buggy and so the railroad industry was born.

With the need for more workers in the railroad industry many immigrants arrived in Canada to work on the railroad line, laying tracks across Canada.The majority of these immigrant workers were either Chinese or Irish. As the construction trade grew, so did the Italian population in Canada.

These three countries, Italy, China and Ireland made up the majority of the immigrant population in Canada until after the second World War.

In the mid to late 1960s the immigration population consisted mainly of Italians, Germans, Portuguese and Greeks seeking an opportunity for economic advancement and the chance of a better life. During the 1970s and 1980s the main source of immigration came from Southeast Asia, specifically Hong Kong, Jamaica and Trinidad, Pakistan and various parts of India.

British Columbia is a diverse, multi-cultural province. Many ethnic communities have settled in or around the Vancouver district. Services are available to assist with social programs, area orientation and English language classes.

INFORMATION

• Affiliation of Multicultural Societies of B.C.
385 South Boundary Road,
Telephone: 604-718-2777

ABORIGINAL PROGRAMS

• Aboriginal, Multiculturalism and Immigration Programs
PO Box 9214 Stn Prov Govt, Victoria, B.C., V8W 9J1
Telephone Vancouver Office: 604 660-2203
WEB: http://www.mcaws.gov.bc.ca/amip/

ALLIANCE FRANCAISE OF VANCOUVER

The Alliance Française of Vancouver was founded in 1903 in order to promote the French language and culture. They are a non-profit cultural and educational association managed by a board of directors elected by its members.

6161 Cambie Street, Vancouver, B.C., V5Z 3B2
Telephone: 604-327-0201
WEB: http://www.alliancefrancaise.ca/

CHINESE CULTURAL CENTRE OF GREATER VANCOUVER

This organization provides educational programs, seminars and exhibits through multi-language services.

The cultural centre has many divisions including the Women's committee, a theatre production company and the Dragon Boat Festival Association.

Traditions within the Chinese culture are kept alive through annual events including Chinese New Year festivals, the Dragon Boat Festival and a Mid Autumn Festival among others.

• Vancouver Office
50 East Pender Street, Vancouver, B.C., V6A 3V6
Telephone: 604-658-8850
WEB: http://www.cccvan.com/

• Richmond Office
860-4400 Hazelbridge Way, Richmond, B.C., V6X 3R8
Telephone: 604-658-8875
WEB: http://www.cccvan.com/

CULTURAL CENTRE SOCIETY

)se of the Italian cultural centre is to provide recreational, id educational support to seniors and youth alike. At this time there are 33 Italian - Canadian associations affiliated with the centre.

3075 Slocan St. Vancouver, B.C., V5M 3E4
Telephone: 604-430-3337
Web: http://www.iccs.bc.ca

LA BOUSSOLE, CENTRE FRANCOPHONE DU DOWNTOWN EASTSIDE

La Boussole is a centre for French-speaking residents of Vancouver and the Downtown Eastside. La Boussole is used as an information drop-in centre and offers assistance with welfare, housing and employment. English courses are also offered as well as translations, literary assistance, social activities, telephone services, temporary storage for certain items, advocacy issues and more.

504 East Broadway Vancouver, B.C., V5T 1X5
Telephone: 604-683-7337

LE CENTRE CULTUREL FRANCOPHONE DE VANCOUVER

The French language community centre offers scheduled activities and a library to those who are members. Other venues to enhance the cultural aspect for the Francophone community include a French festival, a movie festival, a book fair, shows and theatre.The centre publishes an informative newsletter every 3 months.

1551 W. 7th Ave. Vancouver, B.C., V6J 1S1
Telephone: 604-736-9806
Web: http://www.ccfv.bc.ca

SOUTH AFRICAN SOCIETY OF B.C.

The S.A.S. is a not for profit organization which assists South African Expatriates with all immigration, resettling and social needs. In addition to this the S.A.S. organizes social functions within the Greater Vancouver Area to augment networking of expatriates and provide a support base for new immigrants.

Telephone: 604-922-4785
WEB: http://www.sacbd.com/sasbc/

B.C. CIVIL LIBERTIES ASSOCIATION

The B.C. Civil Liberties Association (BCCLA) is the oldest and most active civil liberties group in Canada. They are a group of citizens who volunteer their time and talents to fulfill their mandate to preserve, defend, maintain and extend civil liberties and human rights in British Columbia and across Canada.

WEB: http://www.bccla.org/

DID YOU KNOW

That the Totem Pole which sits outside of British Columbia's Maritime Museum was completed during British Columbia's centennial year, 1958.
The 100-foot pole is an exact replica of one shipped to the UK and presented to Queen Elizabeth.
Both poles were carved by Mongo Martin in Kwakiutl style.
At the top is a chief standing on a beaver.

CHAPTER 10: BUSINESS

CANADIAN BUSINESS CULTURE

Business meals are popular. A business lunch generally lasts about 1 1/2 hours. Breakfast meetings are becoming popular.When invited to a dinner party wait for the host to start talking business. Canadians usually prefer to have business meals outside of their home.

Receiving an invitation to one's home is considered an honour. It is considered rude to be any more than 30 minutes late. Bring flowers for the host/hostess and present them to him/her upon arriving at the home. You can also bring a special bottle of wine of liquor if you prefer.

At the dinner table the host/hostess generally begins eating before the guests. Offer others the main dishes before you serve yourself

Forks are held in the right hand and used for eating. Knives are used to cut or spread something onto a food. To use your knife, switch the fork to your left hand or put it down.The fork is switched back to the right hand to continue eating. If you prefer you may eat in the "continental style" that is, not transferring the fork to your other hand to eat. To signal that you have finished the meal, the knife and fork are laid together on your plate.

Canadians do not consider it rude to refuse to eat a food item. Simply say "no thank you" when offered. Hosts/hostesses appreciate you taking the time after your visit to call or send a note thanking them for their hospitality.

A firm handshake is used as a greeting or introduction in business situations. Men usually wait for women to offer their hand first. An open, cordial manner is the norm when dealing with Canadian business people. Direct eye contact is acceptable, especially when you want to convey interest and sincerity.

The British background that has played a large part in the growth of Canada up to now affects how we participate in social situations. Canadians are generally reserved and some people perceive this to be snobbish. The culture on the West Coast of Canada is more relaxed and social events are not so restrictive.

Canadians in general are open and tolerant. It is considered rude to boast or act ostentatious. Emotions are reserved in public situations. Canadians prefer not to cause a scene in public and will try to be tactful when dealing with people. Speaking in a foreign language in the presence of someone who does not understand that language is considered rude.

Smoking is a health concern for many people which has resulted in public venues banning smoking. The city of Vancouver and surrounding municipalities of the Greater Vancouver Regional District (GVRD) have some of the toughest anti smoking bylaws in Canada.

Laws recently introduced allow hospitality and gaming establishements to permit smoking on their premises. They must have separate rooms for smoking and non-smoking patrons. Smoking rooms must be structurally separate and can be no more than 45% of total floor space in hospitality settings and 65% in bingo halls.

DID YOU KNOW

That the Port of Vancouver handles nearly 10,000 vessels each year, of which 3,000 are foreign ships from some 90 nations. With more than 20 major cargo and marine-related facilities handling between 65 and 70 million tonnes annually, Vancouver is the top export port on the North American west coast. As the most diversified port in the Western Hemisphere, Vancouver handlescoal, grain, potash, sulphur, mineral concentrates, petroleum products, liquid chemicals, lumber, pulp, paper, woodchips, containers and cruise ships.

BUSINESS IN GREATER VANCOUVER

Vancouver serves as the corporate headquarters for British Columbia's business community. The Canadian Venture Exchange, similar to the TSE and NYSE, is located here. Additionally, 30 foreign banks, 15 international financial institutions and major branch offices of the largest chartered banks in Canada make Vancouver their base.

The city is one of two designated International Financial Centres in Canada, the other being the city of Toronto. This designation carries with it important tax benefits for businesses engaged in certain types of international commerce.

Vancouver's rapidly expanding service and high technology sectors are reshaping the region's economic composition. Once heavily based on forestry, fishing, mining and transportation, Vancouver's economy is now dependant on high technology and knowledge based industries.

Telecommunications, electronics and information technology are the fastest growing industries in the city's knowledge based manufacturing sector.

New immigrants, particularly from the Pacific Rim, contribute greatly to the entrepreneurial spirit of the city and have added a distinctive international flavour to the business climate.

Most communities have a chamber of commerce. This organization provides business owner/employers an opportunity to get involved in their community, attend seminars and network with other corporate members.

CHAMBERS OF COMMERCE

• B.C. Chamber of Commerce
1201 - 750 West Pender Street, Vancouver, B.C., V6C
Telephone: 604-683-0700
WEB: http://www.bcchamber.org/

• Delta Chamber of Commerce
6201-60th Avenue Delta, B.C., V4K 4E2
Telephone: 604-946-4232
WEB: http://www.deltachamber.com/

• Greater Langley Chamber of Commerce
#1, 5761 Glover Road., Langley, B.C., V3A 8M8
Telephone: 604-530-6656
WEB: http://www.langleychamber.com/

• New Westminster Chamber of Commerce
601 Queens Avenue, New Westminster B.C., V3M 1L1
Telephone: 604-521-7781
WEB: http://www.newwestchamber.com/

• North Vancouver Chamber of Commerce
131 East 2nd Street, North Vancouver, B.C., V7L 1C2
Telephone: 604-987-4488
WEB: http://www.nvchamber.bc.ca/

• Surrey Chamber of Commerce
#101, 14439-104 Avenue Surrey, B.C., V3R 1M1
Telephone: 604-581-7130
WEB: http://www.surreychamber.org/

• Tri-Cities Chamber of Commerce, Serving
Coquitlam, Port Coquitlam, Port Moody
#3 - 1180 Pinetree Way Coquitlam, B.C., V3B 7L2
Telephone: 604-464-2716
WEB: http://www.chamberofcommerce.bc.ca/

NETWORKING

The following web sites will provide you with information on the economic development plans for Vancouver as well as networking opportunites for business owners.

· The Vancouver Board of Trade
Suite 400, 999 Canada Place Vancouver, B.C., V6C 3C1
Telephone: 604-681-2111
WEB: http://www.boardoftrade.com/

· Vancouver Economic Development Commission
608 West Cordova Street Vancouver, B.C., V6B 5A7
Telephone: 604-632-9668
WEB: http://www.vancouvereconomic.com/

· Downtown New Westminster, 125 - 435 Columbia Street
Telephone: 604-524-4996

· The Law Society of British Columbia
845 Cambie Street, B.C. V6B 4Z9
Telephone: 604-669-2533
WEB: http://www.lawsociety.bc.ca/

· Institute of Chartered Accountants of British Columbia
600 - 1133 Melville Street, Vancouver B.C., V6E 4E5
Telephone: 604-681-3264
WEB: http://www.ica.bc.ca/

CHAPTER 11: BANKING

The financial industry in Canada is regulated at a federal level by the Bank of Canada. There are several banking institutions within the Canadian geographic area. However they are all governed by the same federal agency known as the Bank of Canada and must comply to all rules and regulations as stipulated by the Bank of Canada. Banks are not privately owned institutions thus far, as in the United States, but there is a move on to encourage this. Several of the financial institutions would prefer to amalgamate to enhance their strength financially but this is yet to be approved by the government.

Two of the major players attempted a merger a few years ago. The government struck down their request stating that the merger may eventually create a monopoly in the financial industry.

All major banks offer basicallly the same services in different packages across Canada. You can now purchase stocks, insurance, GICs, RRSPs, bonds, travelers insurance, set up automated bill payments and payroll deposits, and of course cash transactions such as deposits, withdrawals and currency exchange.

Canadians are very comfortable with the concept of on-line banking and conduct many of their financial transactions via the Internet. This obviously saves time but in addition, it also provides research information for the person interested in finding out more regarding such things as stocks or mortgage rates etc.

Most banks offer an on-line system for the purchase and sale of stocks.They supply you with an account number, information on how to get set up and then you may buy and sell any stocks you wish. There is generally a transaction fee to do this which tends to be less expensive than the fee a broker would charge for the same service. Although you do not get the expertise of a broker, if you feel confident enough to be responsible for your own portfolio, it is an alternative.

Canadians are also very receptive to the idea of automated teller machines known as ATMs, and debit cards. The debit cards are used in lieu of cash and they are accepted at virtually every retail establishment in the Greater Vancouver Area. Many people prefer to carry their debit card with them instead of carrying cash for the security factors involved.

Every bank offers their own debit card and credit card. Each offers advantages and various service charges so it is best to do your homework and find the financial institution that best fits your needs.

To set upon account at a bank, if you have not had one in Canada before, you will need the following documents and information. The bank may, depending on the circumstances, "hold funds" in your account for a period of time. You will be required to present a Social Insurance Number (SIN) as identification as well as any credit cards you hold.

To "hold funds" means that if you deposit a cheque into your account you will not be able to access these funds until the cheque has cleared, generally 3-5 business days. This is considered a probationary period between you and the bank.

The bank will require you to fill out an application form in order to process your request to open an account. If you have established a credit history in the area you are moving from, the bank may take this into consideration. Banks generally don't look at credit ratings from other countries. There are factors that could change this including such things as home ownership, stock portfolio, company reference or bank reference, so it is advisable to discuss this with the bank manager in the new area.

Quite often a business will have a working relationship with a specific bank which would enable you to establish an account with greater ease. If your company does not suggest a bank to you, ask them which one they use and whether or not they can assist you in setting up an account.

Financial institutions, such as banks, have their head offices in downtown Toronto. Toronto is recognized as the financial centre of Canada. We have included local contact numbers for each of the bank companies.

> The following list is only a partial list of the banks and credit unions in the GVRD. For more information refer to the "yellow pages."

• Bank of Montreal, 595 Burrard St. Vancouver, B.C., V7X 1L7
Telephone: 604-665-2643
WEB: http://www.bmo.com/

• CIBC, 8450 Granville Street, Vancouver, B.C., V6P 4Z7
Telephone: 1-800-465-2422
WEB: http://www.cibc.com/

• HSBC, 2735 Granville Street, Vancouver, B.C., V6H 3J1
Telephone: 604-668-4715
WEB: http://www.hkbc.com/

• RBC Royal Bank, 1497 West Broadway, Vancouver, B.C., V6H 1H7
Telephone: 604-665-5700
WEB: http://www.royalbank.com/

• Scotia Bank, 1 West Broadway, Vancouver, B.C., V5Y 1P1
Telephone: 604-668-3789
WEB: http://www.scotiabank.com/

• TD Canada Trust, 805 West Broadway, Vancouver, B.C., V5Z1K1
Telephone: 604-874-2122
WEB: http://www.tdcanadatrust.com/

• Coast Capital Savings Credit Union
1075 West Georgia St.Vancouver, BC, V6E 3C9
Telephone: 604-682-7728
WEB: http://www.coastcapitalsavings.com/

• Gulf and Fraser Credit Union
803 East Hastings Street,Vancouver, BC, V6A 1R8
Telephone: 604-254-9811
WEB: http://www.gulfandfraser.com/

• North Shore Credit Union
1080 Marine Drive North Vancouver, BC, V7P 1S5
Telephone: 604 903-2420
WEB: http://www.nscu.com/

• Van City Savings Credit Union
501 West 10th Avenue, Vancouver, BC, V5T 2A3
Telephone: 604-877-7000
WEB: http://www.vancity.com/

• Westminster Savings Credit Union
6108 - 2850 Shaughnessy Street, Port Coquitlam, BC, V3C 6K5
Telephone: 604-942-6691
WEB: http://www.wscu.com/

CANADIAN CURRENCY

The Canadian monetary system is similar to the American system. That is we use dollars and cents. Unlike the United States, Canadian currency has different colours for different denominations of bills. Americans often refer to our money as Monopoly money because of the colours.

The Canadian dollar bill and two dollar bill are no longer in circulation. These have been replaced by coins.

The one dollar coin is affectionately known as the 'loonie' because of the loon symbol on the face of it. The loon is a very symbolic bird in Canada. It frequents the waters and wetlands of the northern regions. This enchanting bird is very graceful in the water and has distinctive markings on its body. The cry of the loon is quite often referred to as "haunting, mysterious or mystical".

The two dollar coin is generally referred to as a "toonie." (rhymes with loonie, no other reason really) The toonie can be distinguished from the loonie by the patented coin locking mechanism integrated into the coin connecting two metals together. This makes the toonie look like it has a smaller coin set inside the centre of a larger coin.

The five, ten, twenty, fifty, one hundred and five hundred dollar bills are still in circulation. In May 2000 the Bank of Canada began to withdraw the $1,000.00 note in an effort to reduce money laundering and the manufacturing of counterfeit bills.

The Canadian Loonie has become famous since the Winter Olympics held in Salt Lake City. The story goes that the gentleman in charge of preparing the ice for the playoff hockey games buried a loonie into the ice for good luck. It worked, both our women and men's hockey teams took the gold medal. This loonie is now on display at the Hockey Hall of Fame in Toronto.

At the present time the value of the Canadian dollar is equal to approximately 55% of the American dollar. This means that an American traveling to Canada will receive at least $1.55 Canadian for every American dollar that they change. Rates will vary somewhat depending on where you try to cash them. Financial institutions will usually offer the same rate; retail outlets and restaurants usually offer less to purchase your money. In other words, at a bank you may receive $ 1.50 per American dollar, at a retail outlet it may be as low as $ 1.40 per American dollar.

The same applies for any of the world's major currencies, so exchanging your money in a bank or credit union will lower your costs.

CHAPTER 12: EDUCATION

GENERAL OVERVIEW

Education is an essential element of the Canadian culture and a focus on continuing education is a common goal among Canadian families. Students may enter the school system between the ages of 4-6, on a voluntary basis, but must be enrolled by the time they have reached the age of 6. Students are encouraged to remain in school until at least the age of 18.

Many families urge their children to further their education at a post-secondary institution. The public and separate (Catholic) education programs at both the elementary level and secondary level are free for residents of British Columbia. Private schools are not funded by the government and the annual fees vary from school to school.

The Ministry of Education in British Columbia sets the curriculum throughout the B.C. public school system. This ensures that students in any part of British Columbia will receive the same educational opportunities regardless of residence.

School holidays are generally the same for all school systems that are not independently operated. Schools are closed over the Christmas holiday and Easter holiday. Students do not attend school during the summer months of July and August.

Private schools may offer their own school holidays, with longer breaks. They begin their school year sooner, have longer class time, and end the school season sooner than the public system.

All school boards offer teachers professional or academic days during the school year. This is an opportunity for the teaching community to enhance their skills, attend workshops and seminars and keep current on innovative new teaching methods.

Students do not attend school on these professional development days. This is also the time that teachers use to meet with parents to discuss report cards and academic achievements of their children. There are six days per year set aside for this.

Schools within both the urban and suburban school areas are usually within walking distance for most children. Children in rural areas are almost always bussed in and the students in the urban and/or suburban areas may be bussed, depending on board policy. It is best to ensure the Board does offer transportation for students and the criteria for this service, as costs for bussing are becoming prohibitive in some areas. Your school board will be able to provide you with the information regarding bussing services, boundary guidelines etc.

There are 90 elementary schools within the Greater Vancouver Area and 18 secondary schools. Attending a public school is free to any child legally residing in the Greater Vancouver Area.

An alternative to attending the standard schools is the option of home schooling. This is becoming more popular each year. The students must adhere to the same curriculum as set by the Ministry. Testing is done to ensure proper cirriculum is being taught.

The Greater Vancouver Area education system also has a French as a first language school board and a Catholic school board.

The Catholic school system is partially funded by the provincial and municipal governments to a maximum of 50%. The balance of the funding is raised by the parish community through tuition fees paid by the parents and fund-raising efforts throughout the parish community.

Currently the Catholic Independent Schools of the Greater Vancouver Area have forty elementary and nine secondary schools with plans for three additional secondary schools in the near future.

Francophones are provided with French as a first language schools at both the elementary and secondary levels. This is a government funded program so tuition fees are not applicable. The federal and provincial governments, having ensured these provisions were in place, have demonstrated an effort to provide Francophones within the Greater Vancouver Area an opportunity to pursue their cultural diversity, heritage and native language.

REGISTRATION

PUBLIC SCHOOL

Registration in the Greater Vancouver area public school district is done at the neighbourhood school or at the District Reception and Placement centre, depending on the circumstances.

Most students are eligible to register directly at their neighbourhood school. If a student was born in Canada, but outside of Vancouver, and English is their second language, or if a student was born outside of Canada and English is their first language, they must register at the District Reception and Placement Centre.

During the summer months, when schools are not open, students who speak English as a first language and were born in Canada must register at the District Reception and Placement Centre.

Make an appointment to register at the school. You will have to have your child's birth certificate, proof of residence (rental or purchase agreement) school report cards from the previous two years and important health and immunization information.

If your child was born in Canada, but outside of Vancouver and English is not the first language spoken, you will need to register at the District Reception and Placement Centre (DRPC) You must bring one of the following with you to the appointment:

• parent's authorization for employment
• parent's student authorization
• parent's diplomatic visa

In addition to this identification you must also bring important immunization information and health issues, school report cards from the last two years and proof of residence (rental/purchase agreement.)

• Vancouver School Board
1580 West Broadway
Telephone: 604-713-5000
WEB: http://www.vsb.bc.ca/

REGISTRATION

CATHOLIC SCHOOL

Your family is considered a member of the parish if you are:

- Registered in the parish
- Regularly attending Mass at the parish
- Use Sunday envelopes from the parish on a regular basis.
- Participate in the work activities required of you by the parish

All schools have a uniform policy. Most schools have a participation policy for both students and parents of the parish. A monetary levy is assessed to families choosing not to participate.

Individual schools handle their own registrations. Because of the high demand for Catholic education, most of the schools are full, with waiting lists. For further information, or application to an individual school, please contact the school directly.

- Catholic Independent Schools
150 Robson Street, Vancouver, B.C., V6B 2A7
Telehone: 604-683-9331
Web: http://cisva.rcav.org/

VANCOUVER SCHOOL STATISTICS

Public Schools Elementary School Enrollment 12,140
Secondary School Enrollment 8,507
Number of High School Graduates 1,219
Student Teacher Ratios:
Elementary School Enrollment 17.3 %
Secondary School Enrollment 15.9 %

148

PRIVATE SCHOOLS

There are numerous private schools within the Greater Vancouver Area. The demand for private education in British Columbia is increasing due to a change in the funding focus by the provincial Ministry of Education. This has led many people who reside in the GVA to consider having their children educated in the private school system which, in turn, has caused some of the schools to be at their maximum capacity for enrollment.

If you wish your child to attend a private school, be certain that there is enough space to accommodate them. Remember, one of the reasons children are enrolled in private schools is because of the smaller numbers of students in the classroom. The teacher/student ratio is lower than the provincial average for public schools. Private schools will not compromise this condition for enrollment.

There are schools that board students and schools that transport students on a daily basis to and from the school. Some are neighbourhood children, some are bussed in from other neighbourhoods. Private schools can be co-ed, male only or female only. There are schools for various age groups, beginning at age 4 and continuing up to the last academic year of high school (usually age 18 or 19 in British Columbia.)

BC HOMESCHOOL ASSOCIATION

It has only been in the last decade or two that parents are reviewing the quality of education that their children are receiving in the "traditional" school setting and the environment in which it is being administered.
The reasons to assume the responsibility to home school are varied, but one thing is certain, this educational option is here to stay!

WEB: http://www.bchomeschool.org/

GREATER VANCOUVER AREA SCHOOL DISTRICTS

• Vancouver School Board
1580 West Broadway,
Telephone: 604-713-5000
WEB: http://www.vsb.bc.ca/

• West Vancouver School District
1075-21st Street, West Vancouver, B.C., V7V 4A9
Telephone: 604-981-1000
WEB: http://www.sd45.bc.ca

• North Vancouver School Board
721 Chesterfield Ave, North Vancouver, B.C., V7M 2M5
Telephone: 604-903-3444
WEB: http://www.nvsd44.bc.ca/

• Richmond School Board
7811 Granville Avenue, Richmond, B.C., V6Y 3E3
Telephone: 604-668-6000
WEB: http://www.sd38.bc.ca/

• School District No.43 (Coquitlam)
550 Poirier Street, Coquitlam B.C., V3J 6A7
Telephone: 604-939-9201
WEB: http://www.sd43.bc.ca/

• Catholic Independent Schools
150 Robson Street, Vancouver, B.C., V6B 2A7
Telehone: 604-683-9331
Web: http://cisva.rcav.org/

• Langley School District
4875 - 222 Street, Langley B.C., V3A 3Z7
Telephone: 604- 534-7891.
WEB: http://www.sd35.bc.ca/

• Francophone Schools
Conseil scolaire francophone de la Colombie-Britannique
180-10200 Shellbridge Way, Richmond, B.C., V6X 2W7
Téléphone: 604-214-2600
WEB: http://www.csf.bc.ca/

GREATER VANCOUVER PRIVATE SCHOOLS

• Collingwood School
70 Morven Drive, West Vancouver
Telephone: 604-925-3331
WEB: http://www.collingwood.org/

• Crofton House (Girls School)
3200 West 41st Avenue, Vancouver
Telephone: 604 263-3255
WEB: http://www.Croftonhouse.bc.ca/

• Meadowridge School
12224 - 240th Street, Maple Ridge,
Telephone: 604-467-4444
WEB: http://www.meadowridge.bc.ca/

• Mulgrave School
2330 Cypress Lane, West Vancouver
Telephone: 604-922-3223
WEB: http://www.mulgrave.com/

• St. Georges (Boys School)
Senior School: 4175 West 29th Avenue
Telephone: 604-224-1304

• Junior School:3851 West 29th Avenue
Telephone: 604-224-4361
WEB: http://www.stgeorges.bc.ca/

• Vancouver Waldorf School
2725 St. Christopher's Road, North Vancouver
Telephone: 604-985-7435
WEB: http://www.vws.bc.ca/

• York House School (Girl's School)
4176 Alexandra St., Vancouver
Telephone: 604-736-6551
WEB: http://www.yorkhouse.bc.ca/

This is only a partial list of Private Schools in the GVRD.
For more information refer to the "yellow pages."

HIGHER EDUCATION

UNIVERSITY OF BRITISH COLUMBIA

UBC is ranked as one of Canada's top medical/doctoral universities, though teaching and research are conducted in all disciplines at UBC. UBC receives upwards of $165 million annually in research funding from government, industry, and foundations. Faculty members conduct more than 4,000 research projects annually.

• The University of British Columbia
2329 West Mall Vancouver, B.C., V6T 1Z4
Telephone: 604-822-2211
WEB: http://www.ubc.ca/

SIMON FRASER UNIVERSITY

SFU is rated as one of Canada's top comprehensive universities by Maclean's Magazine. The university has two campuses one in downtown Vancouver and one in Burnaby. As a "comprehensive" university, SFU has programs in the liberal and fine arts, sciences, applied sciences, business, education and cooperative education.

• Simon Fraser University
8888 University Drive, Burnaby, B.C., V5A 1S6
Telephone: 604-291-3111
WEB: http://www.sfu.ca/

BRITISH COLUMBIA INSTITUTE OF TECHNOLOGY

BCIT is an innovative province-wide organization specializing in advanced technology training. The focus in on those initiatives that increase economic and entrepreneurial activity and employment in the province. BCIT offers a Bachelor of Technology degree in Computer Systems Technology and Environmental Engineering Technology.

• British Columbia Institute of Technology
3700 Willingdon Avenue, Burnaby, B.C., V5G 3H2
Telephone: 604-434-5734
WEB: http://www.bcit.ca/

THE SCHOOL OF COMMUNICATION

 The School of Communication offers diverse theoretical and applied approaches to media, technologies, and culture in a rapidly changing global context and from an array of interdisciplinary perspectives.
They are committed to the pursuit of innovative teaching, cutting edge research, and the constant interplay of knowledge and practice.

• The School of Communication
8888 University Drive, Burnaby, B.C., V5A 1S6
Telephone: 604-291-3687
WEB: http://www.sfu.ca/communication/

EMILY CARR INSTITUTE OF ART & DESIGN

 Emily Carr is becoming more of an international institution with students from more than twenty countries as well as having exchanges with all major art schools. Emily Carr recently launched a new Centre for Art and Technology .The centre's first director is Carol Gigliotti. The Centre for Art and Technology will allow everyone at Emily Carr to explore art, technology and creativity.

• Emily Carr Institute of Art + Design
1399 Johnston Street, Granville Island
Vancouver, B.C, V6H 3R9
Telephone: 604-844-3800
WEB: http://www.eciad.bc.ca/

VANCOUVER COMMUNITY COLLEGE

 Vancouver Community College is situated against a backdrop of snow-capped mountains and the sparkling Pacific Ocean. Vancouver Community College has been a vibrant educational facility for more than 30 years.

• Vancouver Community College
1155 East Broadway, Vancouver B.C., V5N 5T9
Telephone: 604-443-8300
WEB: http://www.vcc.bc.ca/

CHAPTER 13: USEFUL INFORMATION

MEASURING UP: METRIC AND IMPERIAL

Canadians have embraced the European standard of metric measurement for temperature, weight, height etc. since its introduction to the school system in the 1970s. However, there are still many people who prefer to use the "'old'" style of measurements, that is pounds and inches also known as the imperial standard of measurement based on English standards.

Here is a smidgen of information for you on metric conversions....

All students study in metric and Celsius measurements.

• A Canadian gallon is different than an American gallon.
• A Briton weighing 8 stone, a Canadian weighing 55.9 kilograms and an American weighing 123 pounds are all the same weight.
• An American fluid ounce is equal to 1.0408 fluid ounces in the United Kingdom which is equal to 29.574 milliliters in Canada.

• In the United States when it is 30 degrees outside it is very cold, in Canada when it is 30 degrees outside it is very hot. Thirty degrees Celsius is approximately 90 degrees Fahrenheit.

The use of metric measurements can cause some confusion when listening to such things as weather reports, buying gas for the vehicle or selecting a steak at the local butchers.

For example if you were to listen to the weather report before you left for a shopping trip to the grocery store and heard that the temperature was 28 degrees you would probably grab your coat and gloves to keep you warm if you did not realize that the weather person was referring to 28 degrees Celcius. 28 degrees Celcius converts into 82 degree Fahrenheit.

Most grocery items in the Vancouver area are labeled in both metric and imperial. If you do need to order something from the delicatessen counter, the price per unit will display both metric and imperial weight. It is also interesting to note that since British Columbia is bilingual all items must be labeled in both English and French.

GOVERNMENT CONTACTS

· Belcarra Village Office
Telephone: 604-937-4100
WEB: http://www.vob.belcarra.bc.ca/

· Bowen Island Municipal Council
Telephone: 604-947-4255
WEB: http://www.bowen-island-bc.com/

· City of Burnaby
Telephone: 604-294-7944
WEB: http://www.city.burnaby.bc.ca/

· City of Coquitlam
Telephone: 604-927-3000
WEB: http://www.city.coquitlam.bc.ca/

· City of Langley
Telephone: 604-514-2800
WEB: http://www.city.langley.bc.ca/

· City of New Westminster
Telephone: 604-521-3711
WEB:http://www.city.new-westminster.bc.ca/

· City of North Vancouver
Telephone: 604-985-7761
WEB: http://www.cnv.org/

· City of Port Moody
Telephone: 604-469-4500
WEB: http://www.cityofportmoody.com/

· City of Port Coquitlam
Telephone: 604-927-5411
WEB: http://www.city.port-coquitlam.bc.ca/

· City of Richmond
Telephone: 604-**276-4000**
WEB: http://www.city.richmond.bc.ca/

• City of Surrey
Telephone: 604-591-4011
WEB: http://www.city.surrey.bc.ca/

• City of Vancouver
Telephone: 604-873-7011
WEB: http://www.city.vancouver.bc.ca/

• City of White Rock
Telephone: 604-541-2100
WEB: http://www.city.whiterock.bc.ca/

• Delta Municipal Hall
Telephone: 604-946-4141
WEB: http://www.corp.delta.bc.ca/

• District of Maple Ridge
Telephone: 604-463-5221
WEB: http://www.district.maple-ridge.bc.ca/

• District of Pitt Meadows Municipal Hall
Telephone: 604-465-5454
WEB: http://www.pittmeadows.bc.ca/

• Greater Vancouver Regional District, (GVRD)
Telephone: 604-432-6200
WEB: http://www.gvrd.bc.ca/

• Village of Anmore
Telephone: 604-469- 9877
WEB: http://www.anmore.com/

• West Vancouver Municipal Hall
Telephone: 604-925-7000
WEB: http://www.westvancouver.net/

• Government of B.C.
Enquiry B.C., Provincial Call Centre
Telephone: 604-660-2421
WEB: http://www.gov.bc.ca/

• Government of Canada
Telephone: 1-800-622-6232
WEB: http://canada.gc.ca/

NEWSPAPERS

• The Province, 200 Granville Street
Telephone: 604-605-2000
WEB: http://www.canada.com/vancouver/theprovince/

• The Vancouver Sun, 200 Granville Street
Telephone: 604-605-2000
WEB: http://www.canada.com/vancouver/vancouversun/

• North Shore News, 1139 Lonsdale Avenue
Telephone: 604-985-2131
WEB: http://www.nsnews.com/

TV/RADIO

• BC CTV
Telephone: 604-608-2868
WEB: http://www.vancouvertelevision.com/

• CKNW 980AM
Telephone: 604-331-2711
WEB: http://www.cknw.com/

• CKVU-TV
Telephone: 604-876-1344
WEB: http://www.ckvu.ca/

• Fairchild Radio (Chinese)
Telephone: 604-708-1234
WEB: http://www.fm961.com/

• Global TV
Telephone: 604-420-2288
WEB: http://www.canada.com/vancouver/globaltv/

• 99.3 The FOX
Telephone: 604-684-7221
WEB: http://www.cfox.com/

INTERNET SERVICE PROVIDERS

• Axion Internet Communications Inc.
Telephone: 604-687-8030
WEB: http://www.axionet.com

• PrismNet
Telephone: 604-270-7135
WEB: http://www.iprism.com/

• UNIServe
Telephone: 604-856-6281
WEB: http://www.uniserve.com/

BOOKSTORES

• Banyen Books & Sound
2671 Broadway West Vancouver
Telephone: 604-732-7912
WEB: http://www.banyen.com/

• Duthie Books, 2239 West Fourth Ave.
Telephone: 604-732-5344
WEB: http://duthiebooks.com/

Other books in the Relocation 101: series:
Relocation 101: Focus on the Greater Toronto Area
ISBN: 0-9688686-6
Relocation 101: Focus on the Greater Victoria Area
ISBN: 155369097-4
Relocation 101: Focus on Montreal
ISBN: 141200059-9

ORDER THEM HERE

WEB: http://relocation101.ca

158

SERVICES FOR SENIORS

• Britannia Community Centre Vietnamese Seniors Program
Telephone: 604-718-5815

• Chinese Community Library Seniors Outreach Program
Telephone: 604-254-2107

• Japanese Community Voluntary Association
Telephone: 604-687-2171

• Jewish Family Seniors Outreach
Telephone: 604-257-5151

• Marpole Oakridge Seniors Council
Telephone: 604-266-5301

• Renfrew Collingwood Seniors Society
Telephone: 604-430-1441

• South Granville Seniors Centre/Spanish Outreach
Telephone: 604-732-0812

• South Vancouver Seniors Network
Telephone: 604-324-6212

• Success Seniors Outreach Project
Telephone: 604-684-1628

• Vancouver Second Mile Society
Telephone: 604-254-2194

• Westend Seniors Network
Telephone:604-669-5051

• Office for Seniors
B.C. Ministry of Health Services
Telephone: 250-952-1238
WEB:
http://www.healthservices.gov.bc.ca/bchealthcare/seniors.html

• CARP, Canada's largest 50+ advocacy group
WEB: http://www.fifty-plus.net/

INDEX

INDEX